Kev F Sutherland is a comic writer and artist whose work appears in The Beano, Doctor Who Adventures, Women Of The Bible, Marvel comics and many more. On stage, online and on TV he is the man behind the world-famous Scottish Falsetto Sock Puppet Theatre. He presents Comic Art Masterclasses in schools, libraries and art centres. He is the creator and executive producer of The Sitcom Trials. Kev also works as a caricaturist, author for TV and radio, Comic Festival producer, comics historian and pundit, stand-up comedian and public speaker. comicfestival.co.uk

Monday, 1 January 2018
My Predictions for 2018 (and how'd I do last time?)

Having enjoyed reading about "Toward The Year 2018", written 50 years ago, I'm minded to do something similar myself.

Last time I tried making any predictions for the year ahead was 2016, when I looked at how badly I'd predicted the previous year, then had some stabs at the next one.

Then I forgot I'd done it, and didn't bother with any predictions for 2017 at all. So, let's have a look at my Jan 2016 predictions, and see how they panned out, given two years to do so. Then we'll make some fresh goes.

In Jan 2016 I wrote **Ten Things I Would Like To See In 2016**:

1 - Donald Trump gets excommunicated by the Republican Party so has to stand as an independent and loses humiliatingly.
- WRONG. So so wrong.

2 - Jeremy Corbyn becomes increasingly popular, winning byelection after byelection and the support of the entire country.
- ALMOST RIGHT. Took till 2017's snap election, but sort of happened.

3 - Steven Moffat passes on the role of Doctor Who showrunner, amicably, and carries on writing new episodes.
- HALF RIGHT. Whether he writes new stories, we have to see.

4 - Drones get strictly regulated following a fatal accident (due, probably, to someone doing something like this).
- NOT YET

5 - ISIS become unpopular among their supporters and just, kind of, fizzle out.
- NOT QUITE YET, but the process could be starting (lots of articles from 2015 through 2017 suggest they're losing popularity, yet they linger)

6 - BBC Four runs out of 1970s pop groups to make documentaries about.
- WRONG. The spring 2018 season is full of them.

7 - Eastenders goes a whole year with no-one dying.
- VERY WRONG. Two years later, the undertakers have been doing a roaring trade. 8 deaths in 2016, 4 in 2017.

8 - Marvel superhero movies go all unpopular and plans are announced not to make any more (for a while).
- WRONG, though this could still lie ahead.

9 - There won't be a referendum or general election of any sort in the UK.
- TOTALLY WRONG. Brexit in 16, snap election in 17.

10 - Fingers crossed 2016 will be less terroristy than 2015, and we're all happy and bright by the end of it.
- SORT OF RIGHT. In 2016 it was celebrities who died in abundance, the UK had the death of Jo Cox but no major incidents. Sadly 2017 made up for that with Manchester Arena, Westminster Bridge, Borough Market and other attempts.

And so to **Ten Things That Could Happen in 2018 For Better Or Worse**:

The Republicans do well in the mid-terms, strengthening Trump's power

Theresa May clings to power and even wins a byelection

The new **Doctor Who** sees its best ratings successes of the decade

Strictly contestants include Steph off of BBC Breakfast and a former Doctor Who

Brexit gets softer as the year progresses, and its deadline gets moved

Flying car goes on the market

Netflix suffers major financial blow

and cuts lots of programmes

Price of litre of petrol goes up (from £1.20 to £1.30)

Average house price falls (from £225K to £215K)

Old TV show revivals: Rainbow, El Dorado, Catweazle, Quatermass

Let's see shall we? Here's to a sunny and bright 2018

Predictions for 2016
Predictions for 2015
Predictions for 2014
Predictions for 2012/13
Predictions for 2011
Predictions for 2010

PS: This is an interesting set of predictions, following on from a thing I posted yesterday "Toward 2018" a book written 50 years ago. What none of them predict is the really big unpredictables, inevitably. The 1968 book still talked about technologies that would affect the press & newspapers, never guessing that paper communication would become a thing of the past. Similarly this set includes "TV becomes extinct", which may well be the case, but the devil is in the detail.

It's always healthy to look at the things nobody predicted, from the last 10 - 50 years. Feminism, LGBT, race and human rights awareness would be the biggest advances I've seen. And smartphones and, in particular, the way we use them. Who could have predicted we would share our thoughts, photos, location etc, in an Orwellian thought police way? Well, I suppose Orwell did, but you know what I mean.

Anyhoo, it'll be fun to look back on these predictions, like seeing a 50 year old Tomorrows World, and laughing. Let us see.

Friday, 5 January 2018
Ruth & Rahab Work In Progress

Continuing my Work In Progress time sheet (started in December) for the two strips from Women Of The Bible, Book Of Ruth and Rahab.

To recap:
Feb 2 2017 - Book Of Ruth script delivered
Apr 20 2017 - Rahab & Jael Wife Of Heber scripts delivered
Dec 1 2017 - Jael Wife Of Heber art delivered (art & colour, just under 1 page per day)
Dec 22 2017 - Ruth 12 pages pencilled (at 4 pages per day)
Jan 4 2018 - Ruth 12 pages inked (at 4.8 pages per day)

Friday Jan 5th midday - Ruth 12 pages, all line art & lettering assembled, ready for colouring. (Assembling and tidying 12 pages of line art took approx 8 hours) PM - Rahab, all 9 pages laid out. Plus, as a bonus, I drew and inserted 3 new panels into Book Of Esther:

Sat & Sun Jan 6 & 7, Rahab voice bubbles laid out and Page 2 pencilled.
Mon Jan 8, 10am - 6pm, Rahab pages 1, 3, 4 and 5 pencilled. 7pm - 11pm p6 and 2/3rds of p7 pencilled.
Tues Jan 9, 10am - 1pm, lots of time spent insuring the car and starting Garda Vetting for Irish schools, p7 and 8 pencilled. 3pm - 6pm, lots more Garda Vetting nonsense, page 9 pencilled. 7pm - 10pm all 9 pages borders & bubbles inked.
Weds Jan 10, 10am - 1pm, pages 2, 4 & 9 inked. 7 - 10pm pages 1, 3, 5 - 7 inked.
Thurs Jan 11, 9.30 - 10.30 (at Peugeot garage) page 8 (final

page) inked. 1pm - 5pm, all pencil erased, pages scanned, assembled ready for colouring.

So Rahab 9 pages pencilled and inked in 4 and a half days, that's 2 pages per day.

Work in progress

Friday, 5 January 2018

In praise of the Fudenosuke Brush Pen

The first week of 2018 has seen a small revolution in my comic strip artwork since I've discovered a new drawing tool - the Tombow Fudenosuke Brush Pen. I bought it between Christmas and New Year at the stationers on Park Street, having failed to find what I was looking for at a shop in Cardiff.

It turned out to be so good that, as I was halfway through my first page using it, I immediately ordered two more, not knowing how long they'd last. Have a look at the photo above. Can you see how, in the first instance, I had a little difficulty knowing what to reorder? That's right, everything is in Japanese.

Added to which, it's only having uploaded the picture above that I realise I've actually ordered the wrong pens. I've just been using the Soft pen and have ordered two Hard pens. When they arrive I'll see whether they're any use. (The difference between soft and hard, as far as the exterior of the pen is concerned, seems to be a slight difference in the pastel shade of two of the 4 boxes on the side. Boy, they certainly want to shift units in English speaking countries, don't they?)

Here's what the end result comes out like...

You might not be able to see a difference between this and my recent stuff, but it's giving me a much finer line than my ink and brush work has been achieving of late. And by god it's faster. So much faster that I've completed my latest job, Book Of Ruth, at the rate of nearly 5 pages a day, with much more detail than previous jobs. And I've so got up to speed that, this afternoon, I just wrote, pencilled, inked and coloured a three panel patch for Book Of Esther (which I originally delivered nearly a year ago, and which has yet to see print). Here, this now goes on page one...

It'll mean nothing to you, but it greatly improves the start of the story. I hope you're all going to see this Women Of The Bible graphic novel (featuring Esther, Ruth, Rahab and Jael) before too long. It's the best work I've written and drawn in years, and I'm inordinately proud of it.

Friday, 12 January 2018
Masterclassathon A Go Go

Blimey, I've certainly been filling up my diary without realising it. Coming up in half term week, Feb 12 - 16, I have a week of Comic Art Masterclasses, all open to the public. If you wished, you could help spread the word. They are...

Feb 12 - Zion Bristol
Feb 13 - Salisbury Arts
Feb 14 - Baldocks Arts & Heritage Centre, Herts
Feb 15 - Angles Theatre, Wisbech
Feb 16 - Bexleyheath & Erith Libraries (no advert for these, I'm sure they'll take care of themselves)

Consider these well and truly tweeted, let's hope they all sell out.

FIRST GLIMPSE
LEICESTER FEB 17

Tuesday, 16 January 2018
Socks new show - teasers

We've done it before (last time, here, in 2016) and we'll no doubt do it again. We're keeping the name of the new Socks show under wraps until it makes its tentative debut in Leicester on Feb 17th. Here's a first tentative teaser of the advert.

Oh go on then, as it's you, here's another teaser to be going on with. Knock yourself out.

The process of writing the show has begun, in fact it began back last Autumn when I started taking suggestions from folks online and making some random sketches. You never know, some of those might make it into the show. And I'm quite pleased with a couple of the new things I've written. Though, I'll be honest, I'm not sitting on an hour's worth of gold yet, so more writing to be done. I'd best get busy eh.

I take great consolation from reading this, a breakdown of the first Leicester preview of Socks Do Shakespeare in Feb 2016. It went on to become our best show, but in Feb of that year we had hardly any of the material that went on to be the killer stuff. Mostly I was still giving them the previous year's show. Ha ha. Brilliant. Suddenly I feel ahead of the game. See also...
Minging Detectives 1st tryout **Feb 15**
Socks In Space full show **Feb 14**
Socks In Space 1st tryout **Feb 13**
Best of **Feb 12**
On The Telly full show **Feb 11**
5 day run of Goes To Hollywood **Feb 09**

In the meantime, tickets are going nicely for the shows we have lined up so far, so get booking them if you haven't already.
Feb 17 & 24 6.50pm Kayal Leicester
Mar 14 & 15 8pm Dram Glasgow
May 26 3.45pm & May 27 5pm Komedia Brighton

Friday, 19 January 2018
Snow & Wind Stop Play - first kids comics of the year

This week I returned to the chalkface with three days of Comic Art Masterclasses, in the far flung reaches of Newcastle and Hannover. And things didn't get off to the smoothest start, with the weather deciding to come over all wintry. And in January, of all times.

On Thursday I was in Hannover for the first time and, though the morning went smoothly, the afternoon class had to be brought to a halt after half an hour due to a storm (Storm Eleanor I think) which had swept across the UK and was now about to devastate Germany. As it happens, though it was a bit breezy on the way back to the hotel, and out again to their brilliant Sprengel Art Museum (about which

I might write some time), Hannover seems to have been spared the worst of the storm, and normal service was resumed the next morning.

The next day two groups of 6th Graders (that's Year 7 in old money) produced the first two complete day's worth of comics this year. And what nice ones they were, despite one of them ending up with the most hackneyed and dismaying title you can ever get from a group of kids - I Don't Know. This is regularly one of the titles a member of the class will come up with (along with the equally dispiriting LOL, Yolo, and Your Mum), but it rarely wins the group vote. Let's assume they were being ironic shall we? They were nice kids, it being the International School in Hannover, so mostly middle class and well travelled for urchins.

The week's classes began at Ponteland in Newcastle, and the first class of the day was the one that suffered from the weather, in this case snow. The pupils had come by minibus from Bellingham, and some of them were from Kielder, which is up the valley. The valley that was being snowed on.

So it was that, after 30 minutes, they all had to get back in the bus and return to school for fear that they might not be able to later. Thus the front cover, named and produced entirely by me, is all that came of the class. They hadn't even begun to start drawing when they had to go. They have the cover as a souvenir. A second group was found to have an ad hoc 45 minute session with me, and then in the afternoon we managed to complete the whole shebang.

So after 3 days and 6 classes in 2018, I so far have a 66% success rate in actually getting to the end of one.

And so far this year 20% of children have chosen Donald Trump as the celebrity to appear in my demonstration strip. Of the 5 classes who got that far, the celebs chosen were Donald Trump, Barack Obama, Dracula, Kim Kardashian and Justin Bieber. All par for the course so far.

Monday, 22 January 2018
Who in Ireland wants a Comic Art Masterclass this week?

(*UPDATE: All sorted. On Wednesday, the marvellous Sarah Purcell, librarian at Margaret Aylward College, intervened and lined me up with a half day of classes on Thursday at Beneavin College in Finglas. So, hooray, I wasn't left thumb-twiddling and did a marvellous if unexpected class with the pupils there. Mother Father kindly disregard this letter).

On Monday I wrote: Does anyone in Ireland want my Comic Art Masterclasses this week? I'm in Dublin right now, doing classes today (Monday 22nd), tomorrow (Tuesday), and Friday 26th. But Wednesday 24th was always going to be free, and now the school I had on Thursday 25th has fallen through

So, are you a school in Ireland? Do you want me to teach your kids how to write and draw comics so that they go away with a comic containing a strip by every one of them, plus an individual caricature by me? Then please get in touch now. Either DM me here, or email kevf.sutherland@gmail.com (and I'll tell you what the costs are).

I can work with two groups in a day, with up to 30 in each group, aged 7 and upwards. I need a minimum of two hours with each group. Please feel free to ask the JCSP Librarians at the schools listed below for what I hope will be glowing recommendations.

Yours with fingers crossed

Kev F Sutherland
Comic Art Masterclasses

Monday, 22 January 2018
Newcastle, Hannover, Dublin, the week of the cancelled classes

January 2018 will, hopefully, go down on the record as my worst hit-rate for actually completing Comic Art Masterclasses. So far 25% of the classes I've set out to deliver have ended up not happening.

First of all, on a one day trip to Ponteland near Newcastle, I started the day teaching pupils who'd been minibussed in from a nearby school, only to have them leave after 30 minutes because it was snowing up the Kielder valley, whence they came, for fear they might not make it back later. So, out of that day's two classes, only one went the distance.

Then on my two day visit to Hannover, the first morning went fine, only for the first afternoon class to be stopped, again after half an hour, as a storm was lashing Germany and the school had to close down. After two days I was looking at a 50% failure-to-finish-a-class rate. Luckily things improved the next day when, for the first time this year, I completed a full day of two classes. Hooray.

Next stop Ireland. And the Irish trip was to be quite the marathon. Four schools in five days. It was nearly five days, but sadly we failed to find a school that worked a full day on Wednesday (many schools take a half day) and could take my classes. But 4 days of schools, spread over a week, and all in Dublin, was a grand bit of management, and I have the assembled librarians of the JCSP libraries of Dublin to thank for the organisation.

The only spanner in the works was Garda Vetting. Not having been to Ireland since 2016, I've been away while Irish law caught up with the UK and Scotland and started asking schools to supply police criminal clearance for all teaching staff. I got my first CRB check (now called a DBS certificate) way back in 2003 and, though it's a convoluted rigmarole for self-employed freelancers to get in the first place, is simple enough when you've found out how. And now it updates itself every year for a small fee, rather than me having to re-register from scratch every three years, which was the previous set up. I got my first Scottish PVG certificate in 2015, which seemed to be an awful lot easier to arrange.

Garda Vetting, as it's called in Ireland, works the same way in as much as it's a nightmare to try and work out how the hell you're supposed to get it if you're a freelancer. Even less explanation is given as to what a visitor from overseas is required to have. Helpfully the Principal of one of the four schools I was to visit sent me the paperwork to fill out, and then forwarded it to the Garda for me. But time was running out and it looked like the Garda wouldn't get it processed in time for my visit this week.

So I approached the Garda Vetting Bureau directly, and got a response from a very helpful Maurice Nolan at the Bureau who told me, "There would... be no

obligation on a school to require vetting of a guest speaker, musician, etc. who is giving a talk or demonstration at a school on a once-off or very irregular basis." Hooray! Problem solved.

For three quarters of my schools, leastways. Three of my schools, on reading the authoritative decision from the official at the Vetting Bureau, agreed with the words of, let's face it, The Law, and gave my visits the go ahead. At time of writing I've just completed a grand day at St Aidans in Tallaght, and tomorrow I'll be returning to New Cross College in Finglas. Then on Friday I'll be making my debut appearance at Killinarden school in Whitestown.

One school (who shall remain nameless) felt differently. Their

Principal emailed me today to say that the Garda Vetting Bureau's (whose job it is to decide who needs vetted by the Garda Vetting Bureau) "opinion differs greatly from the advice given by our management advisory body" . He goes on to suggest that "the National Vetting Bureau needs to consult with schools' advisory bodies to ensure that there is complete clarity". So in his opinion (and in this instance it is an opinion, rather than, you know, the actual law), the police should consult the school on what the law is.

While we leave them to argue that one out, he concludes "I'm afraid that we cannot proceed with Thursday's workshop". So I have an unpaid day in a hotel in Dublin, twiddling my thumbs (okay, getting on with work, of which I have plenty to do), and my hit-rate for completing classes as planned remains 75%. (The four schools were, of course, going to share the cost of my flights, car, and hotel, as a result of which I'm now commensurately out of pocket on all that*)

*UPDATE: On Wednesday, the marvellous Sarah Purcell, librarian at Margaret Aylward College, intervened and lined me up with a half day of classes on Thursday at Beneavin College in Finglas. So, hooray, I wasn't left thumb-twiddling and did a marvellous if unexpected class with the pupils there. All's well that ends well.

Friday, 26 January 2018
Aga Doo? A week of comics by kids in Dublin

Admit it, isn't this one of the last titles you'd have expected a class of 12 year olds in Dublin in the year 2018 to have chosen as the title for their group comic? But choose it they did, at New Cross College in Finglas, on the second day of my marathon week of classes in Dublin. My thanks go out to the JCSP Librarians of the fair city, especially Martina Flynn at St Aidans who led the co-ordination of the schools. It was quite an undertaking, what with the spectre of waiting for my Garda Vetting to

be processed (about which, more here), but in the end it went swimmingly, and look at the great comics the kids produced.

Day one was at St Aidans themselves, and the Year 1 and 2s excelled themselves in being as archetypically teenaged as one comes to expect. Believe me, The Junkie Mushroom was among the more acceptable titles they came up with.

This picture, taken by Mairead at Killinarden, is a wide shot, showing how wide I currently am. What can I say, travel food!

Here are the comics produced by the pupils at Killinarden. They're in Transition Year, which is the mythical Year With No Name that exists in Irish schools. It's actually 4th year (that'd be Year 10 in England) but they don't call it that. They call it Transition Year, and no-one can ever explain why. Whatever, they came up with Finbar Ye Rat, which was my favourite cover drawing of the week. I do all these cover drawings, so it's a bit sad for me to have a favourite. But I do, so there.

And here was the delightful unexpected bonus day, at Beneavin De La Salle College in Finglas, arranged for me at last minute by one of the other librarians (Sarah at Margaret Sylward) whose school couldn't have me themselves, but who took pity on me after I was cancelled at short notice (by the school who shall remain nameless) and faced an unemployed Thursday in Dublin. As it was I had half a day in school, which was way better than none, and they went away with this cracking comic, and this nifty flipchart. Oh yes, the school isn't pronounced Beneavin as in "rhymes with believing", so the flipchart gag doesn't work. I didn't discover that till it was too late. It's pronounced Be-nevv-in. So now you know too.

The celebrities these 7 groups chose for my demonstration strip were Kim Kardashian (twice), Donald Trump, The Rock, Ronaldo, Hugh Jackman, and Beyonce.

Sunday, 4 February 2018

Carrots, Cucumbers, Zombies - this week's comics by kids

A busy week in schools, with a lot of travelling, saw me delivering my Comic Art Masterclasses in Swansea, Rhos, Birmingham, and, in the instance above, a primary school in Chipping Campden which is in a bit of Gloucestershire so far over it's very nearly in Warwickshire. Between them the four groups over the two days I spent there came up with some very inspiring front cover ideas.

These were also from said school, namely St James & Ebrington,

which has the bizarre distinction of being two different schools, in different villages with different postcodes a five mile drive apart, who maintain the conviction that they are in fact one school. I could never fathom why this is the case, it sounded like Orwellian Double Speak whenever any teacher tried to explain it. But they're two schools that are in fact one school. Go, as they say, figure.

St Josephs in Swansea had me back to teach their year 5s, and have the double distinction of not only being the first school to have already booked me for 2019, but also they were the first school this year to come up with a Donald Trump themed title for their comic. They won't be the last.

Mountain Movers is an organisation working with home-schooled kids for whom I did a one-off class in Rhos, in the South Wales valleys. The reason I've drawn that heavily-dressed kid on the cover is that, for reasons best known to themselves, a clump of the kids insisted on keeping their hoodies and hats on throughout the class, regardless of how warm it was. Home-schooled kids, with whom I've done a number of classes all round the country, are always an interesting bunch. The thing they have in common being their not being used to sitting still and listening. But child-control challenges aside, they did sterling work and were fun to teach.

Whizz Kids are another novel group, which I've worked with before and with whom I'll be working again over the coming months. The kids are all in wheelchairs, hence the name, and some have a variety of physical disabilities. All good to work with, though to be honest this wasn't the easiest class to run, by dint of it sharing an echoey sports hall with a Virtual Reality Gaming experience which the kids were taken out of the class at intervals to go and do, meaning that, for most of the session, I only had a third of the kids in my class together, and no single kid actually got the whole of the Comic Art Masterclass. Whatever, we managed to make a comic at the end of it all, and they had a fun afternoon.

The celebrities these eight groups chose for my demonstration strip were Donald Trump (four times!), Olly Murrs, Simon Cowell, Declan Donnelly, and Ronaldo.

Socks new show - the art takes shape

Having roughed out the look for the images for the new Socks 2018 show, I used the version above and put it into the teaser ads that you might have already seen. But I wasn't happy with it. So I went to a drastic extreme and drafted a line version, and asked Socks fans on Twitter and Facebook what they thought.

It's safe to say the outline version (which I hadn't intended using in black and white, but ran up the flagpole that way) was not as popular as the photo version. At one point it was 4 to 1 in favour of the photo. Added to which, a few people noted that the logo read as "Cock Puppet". So I added a bit more colour, and ran it past people in a couple of stages.

And we were starting to get there. (The logo of the show is still under wraps at this stage, hence the gap, and I haven't addressed the Cock Puppet issue yet). But still important points were being made about a cartoon version being likely to attract kids to the show. So finally I came up with the version that, at time of writing, is the one I'm going with.

It's the version I'm happy with. Now let's see what the world thinks shall we? Show not written, at time of blogging, with first Leicester show just 10 days away. Gulp.

Friday, 9 February 2018
Socks Kickstarter is launched

For the first time, the Scottish Falsetto Socks have launched a Kickstarter campaign to help fund the brand new 2018 show. I've no idea how it'll go, but fingers crossed we can make this year's show a great big biggie. The whole campaign is to be found here, and it's all below. Lots of fab and fun incentives to be had, please spread the word, no contribution is too small.

Earth's funniest footwear, the Scottish Falsetto Sock Puppet Theatre, return to the Edinburgh Fringe with their 10th all-new show, and with your help we want to make it the best ever, and bring it to a town near you afterwards. Hello, we are the Scottish Falsetto Sock Puppet Theatre - And so am I - - And so is he, and we're hoping you've heard of us by now. We've been making people laugh on stage and screen for a decade now (our first Edinburgh show was in 2007). We know a few thousand of you follow us on Facebook and Twitter, and over 100,000 of you watched our videos online last year (the DUP one and a Doctor Who one did particularly well). Even better, about 2000 of you came to see our last Edinburgh show – Socks Do Shakespeare in 2016 – and even more came to see the show when it toured throughout 2017. Socks Do Shakespeare was our most successful show, and the one we're proudest of (though we hope you also liked Socks In Space, Minging Detectives, Boo Lingerie and all the rest), and we want 2018's to be even better. We're going to make a big splash in Edinburgh then tour the show around the country, possibly internationally. And we can do it, with your help.

Why are we going to Edinburgh?
The Edinburgh Fringe is the biggest showcase in the world. It's where we attract some of our biggest, most enthusiastic audiences, and where we get seen

by the promoters who book us for our subsequent tour dates. The chances of our show coming to a venue near you are based on the impact we make in Edinburgh. It's also where we garner fabulous reviews, tempting more theatres to book us. And it's where those lovely people from the TV get to see us, edging the Socks closer to the big audiences we know you'd like to be part of.

What do we want the money for?
Putting a show on at the Edinburgh Fringe gets that little bit more expensive every year. And, once we've paid for our venue hire (we've been invited to the prestigious Gilded Balloon for the tenth year running), our listing in the programmes, our accommodation, the tiniest bit of advertising, our posters, our flyers, and sundry other costs that you forget about until they're upon you, even a small self-contained show like the Scottish Falsetto Socks doesn't have any change from five thousand pounds. And we don't see a penny of any profits till the Autumn.

Firstly, what's the show called?
A good question, and one that we'll be answering when it debuts in

Leicester. But guess what – you'll find out first! Yes, no matter how tiny the bit of help you're able to give us, you'll get the Top Secret Show Title revelation first. You're welcome.

Secondly, what do you get?
Take a look at those rewards (on the right). We've put together some smashing things that you and you alone will get your hands on. We hope you'll lap up a few of these priceless, exclusive goodies and help us make this show a great big biggie! **Thirdly** The astute Socks-followers among you might have noticed that a couple of our past shows (we're thinking of 2015's Minging Detectives and 2014's And So Am I) suffered a little because – and we're letting you into a bit of a behind-the-scenes trade secret here – in order to fund the show, Kev F (our star performer) was also running comic art classes in libraries in Edinburgh during the days. Which meant he had less time to devote to preparing and promoting the show and, on a couple of occasions, was in danger of losing his voice. Which, as you can imagine, is one thing the Scottish Falsetto Socks show can do without. We've never asked for your money quite like this before.

We just know we can prepare and run a better show with a little more financial support at the start. So, in order to devote maximum time to writing, preparing and running the best – and funniest – Socks show you've ever even dreamed of, we would be helped by every penny you're able to cough up to stick in our coffers. Loving you in anticipation

The Scottish Falsetto Sock Puppet Theatre

And so am I

And so is he

INCENTIVES Pledge £10 or more
SUPPORT SOCKS We'll tweet and Facebook our thanks to you, and you get a credit on the Socks websites for as long as these things last Pledge £20 or more
STRETCH SUPPORT SOCKS – BADGE AND POSTER As well as the online thanks and credit above, we'll send you a special Limited Edition "I Support The Socks" badge, and a limited edition signed Socks show poster. (So you can have it before Edinburgh, it will be from a previous Socks show, only a finite number of which were printed) Pledge £30 or more
SHIRT 'N' SOCKS – BADGE, POSTER, T-SHIRT A very special "I Support The Socks" t-shirt will be

yours, as well as your Limited Edition "I Support The Socks" badge and a Socks show poster, +online credits etc. Pledge £50 or more

SHIRT'N'SOCKS PLUS WITH T-SHIRT & VIDEO Inclusion in a special Socks video, mentioning our high-ranking Socks Supporters, will be yours, via Youtube. Plus you get the limited edition badge, t-shirt and poster, and the online goodies as above. Pledge £150 or more
BESPOKE VIDEO STARS + T-SHIRT etc Congratulations, you've just commissioned a Socks video uniquely for you, from your suggestions. Name the subject, namedrop anyone you like, send it as a gift or greeting, and we'll turn you out a little something special. And, of course, you get the limited edition badge, t-shirt and a poster, and a mention in the Sock Supporters video, above. Pledge £250 or more
SPECIAL GUEST STAR Well done, Special Guest Star, you just got yourself mentioned in the show (we can't guarantee in what context, but you'll be in there every night). We'll also produce a Bespoke Video for you (as above), with all the goodies available to all the other categories. The works, in short. Pledge £500 or more

SPONSOR From £500 you're entitled to sponsorship rights. Your company logo will appear on all posters and flyers, as well as getting a mention in the show, and you're entitled to every incentive above, from a Bespoke Video to the badges, posters, t-shirts et al. This won't be sole sponsorship rights. (If anyone wants to discuss serious commercial level sponsorship, up to and including exclusive sponsorship and advertising endorsement, we'll need to talk separately, and before the conclusion of this Kickstarter. No sponsorship offer would exclude or supercede the offers being given to other supporters.)

Saturday, 10 February 2018
Funky Monkey Donkey Dance - a week of comics by kids (& teachers)

This week's visits to schools with my Comic Art Masterclasses took me for the first time to Angmering. No, me neither. It's near Worthing. So Hev & I stayed over in Arundel, which is very pretty, in order that I could be there bright & early the next day. The Badge Monster is a riff on the fact that the kids were smothered in badges, up to 14 per child, which they seem to be awarded with a pathological fervour. My guess is that someone on the staff is related to a badge manufacturer.

This comic was the fruit of my afternoon session with NQTs (Newly Qualified Teachers) in Birmingham, a gig I do every year, and from which they seem to benefit. All part of me getting comics into schools however I can.

If it's Saturday, it must be Dungannon. And today I worked at the arts centre with the longest name yet - The Hill Of O'Neill And Ranfurly House Arts Centre. Crazy name, excellent building, with a couple of ruined towers standing

atop a hill which has been home to a variety of houses and castles and, during the Troubles, a helicopter landing pad. Now there's a state of the art new building, with a very good exhibition telling the history of the town, a viewing tower, and some lovely conference rooms, one of which had my class in. There's also a dome for bigger events, and a visitor centre which I didn't see into. It's all happening in Dungannon.

I've drawn a few flipcharts over the last few weeks, few of them classics, but I don't want them to go unremembered, so here are a couple of fair to middling efforts.

The celebrities these five groups chose for my demonstration strips were Donald Trump (twice), Tom Cruise, Kim Kardashian, and Chris Pratt.

Saturday, 17 February 2018
SUPERHEROES - the new show is revealed

Here, after a tantalising wait, is the title of the new Socks show for Edinburgh 2018 - Superheroes. It premieres in Leicester tonight and the name has now been revealed.

We would love every bit of help we can to take it to Edinburgh, so please please join our Kickstarter campaign. It's here at Kickstarter, and every contribution, however small, will help us make this year's show a great big biggie.

The Scottish Falsetto Sock Puppet Theatre are Superheroes at The Gilded Balloon at the Edinburgh Fringe from August 1st to 26th. Before that you can see previews of the show at:

Feb 17 & 24 6.50pm Kayal Leicester
Mar 14 & 15 8pm Dram Glasgow
Mar 29 - Bath Comedy Festival
May 26 3.45pm & May 27 5pm Komedia Brighton
June 16 - Zion, BristolJuly 13 - Neath

 - with more preview dates to be announced

Join the Socks Superhero Kickstarter campaign and get great exclusives incentives and info

Sunday, 18 February 2018

Dolls, Death and Doo Doo - a bumper week of comics by kids

It's half term and therefore a bumper week for Comic Art Masterclasses. From Monday to Friday I did classes somewhere in the country, with a fair bit of travelling involved. This also being the week of the Scottish Falsetto Sock Puppet Theatre' s first preview of their new show Superheroes, I also had lots of writing, music editing, and prop preparation to do in all the intervening moments. Yet, with so much going on, I found time to colour up the covers of the comics the kids in the classes produced. And, by golly, weren't these two from Baldock Arts & Heritage Centre a pair of corkers?

Two classes at Salisbury Art Centre were another pair of barnstormers, and earned me my first five star reviews. Admittedly only from pupils on the assessment forms that some places have them complete at the end of the session, but delightful all the same:

★★★★★ Kids really enjoyed the workshop - loved taking the comic home and have been pouring* over it all evening...

(*She means poring, but who's going to split hairs)

With sellouts at every other class this week (literally, they were turning them away everywhere from Bristol to Baldock, Salisbury to Erith) Wisbech was a slight disappointment as I found myself at the lovely Angles Theatre working with groups of only eight each time. We could have rolled them into one single group of 16 and they'd still only have been half the size of every other group this week. However it's an ill wind, and this cosy number meant I was able to devote more time to each pupil's work, and when it came to adding their doodles to the front cover, I was able to give those pride of place, as you can see with Pickle Rick. (Oh yeah, some people think the kids actually draw these covers. Of course they don't, I do. The kids come up with the titles. Then you see those small scrawls in the background of every cover? That's their bits.)

On Friday I rounded off the week with libraries in Bexleyheath and Erith, with the quickest opportunity to eat lunch on Erith pier. Who

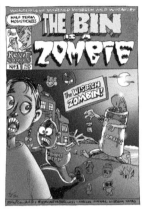

knew there was a pier sticking out into the Thames? Well there is, and pleasant enough it is too. Two more sellout classes were a fine way of rounding off a bumper week.

The week started at Zion Art & Community Centre in Bristol, which is a lovely small operation in a converted chapel on a hill. This was the only class of the week not to have a photocopier, so the kids went away with all the components, but without a finished printed comic. I did all their caricatures as per usual, then laid them out on the floor and photographed them, as you can see above. A fine record, I'm sure you'll agree.

The celebrities these nine groups chose to tread on a worm in my demonstration strip were Donald Trump (a dispiriting 6 times), Jon Bon Jovi, Johnny Depp, and Michael Jackson.

Sunday, 18 February 2018
Superheroes First Preview
Leicester Feb 17 2018

This clip, the closing song from the preview show, is on Youtube as an exclusive clip for Kickstarter supporters. Every else will see it in the fullness of time but not yet.

Scottish Falsetto Socks - Superheroes First Preview Leicester Feb 17 2018

I felt this preview went very well. Leicester are always kind to us, and this was a near-as-dammit sellout so a full house were very supportive of all the new material. And it was mostly new material. Here's what we did and how it went.

For starters we had more than an hour's material, as became clear when I was starting the 10 minute finale with less than 5 minutes to go. But, of course, a lot will change with this show in the coming months.

Intro - **Leicester gags**. 5/10 mostly groans and, of course, no use for any other venue

I'm A Sock Song - 8/10 Good as

always. I was tempted to start with a different song, but I've only ever risked that twice in 10 years and it didn't go well.

Cosmopolitan (mistaken words routine) - 7/10 Good, but could we have something stronger here?

Smell Like Xmas Song - 7/10 Very good song, lots of good laughs, but are audience confused by non-Superhero material starting the show?

The **Christmas/Superhero** misunderstanding - 4/10 not funny to begin with
 - **Batman/Robin/Flash** gags - 7/10 groaners but okay
- **Wonder Woman** visual gag - 4/10 fell flat
- Xmas/Superhero misunderstanding - 4/10 not funny

enough

Motion Capture - 7/10 I love it, but it got mixed reactions. Needs expanding

Nursery Rhymes - 6/10 Getting good laughs with some lines, floppy on others

Peter Parker Song - 6/10 Good, I think will improve

Science - 7/10 Very good laughs, but does it continue well from previous routine?

Horror Song - 0/10 Disaster, the music wasn't on the iPod! Very eggy moment.

1st Appearance of **Brother** - 8/10 Very good.
- Panto good, Cockney Rhyming

Slang very good, great laughs

Racist Brother Song - 7/10 Good, some laughs, will get better. Are audience confused by where the show is going, with so little Superheroes by this stage?

Joker teeth - 8/10 Need more material around it, but good visual

Superman Part 1 - 7/10 No laughs for Jor-El/Kal-El, though I like those bits. Will improve.
More laughs for Ma & Pa Kent.
Glasses - 9/10 Brilliant.

Dead Ringer Song - 8/10 Getting most of its laughs from the glasses, but song will catch up.

Superman gay - 3/10 Not funny

Little Baby Jesus - 5/10 Good laughs and built, could improve if worked in better

Cross Channel Superman - 9/10 Excellent, and will improve.

Split up - 3/10 Needs work

Return of Brother - 6/10 Rhyming Slang and some lines very good, but whole thing loses it way halfway through, not satisfying conclusion. Needs work.

- Captain America costume wasted

All By Myself song - 7/10 Good in parts, maybe needs editing. Piano and drums v good.

Christmas Carol - hard to say as we only did parts, but 8/10 for the parts we did.

Fannying Around Xmas Song - 8/10 Good song, but do we have too much Christmas in the show?

And that was the end of the show. I am worried that I am possibly writing two different shows: A Christmas show and a Superheroes show, each of which has half a show's worth of good material. I may yet have to take the drastic step of separating them out into two shows, which means we'd have Christmas to do in a future year, but that means the weakest material, and the show with the most new writing still needed, is the Superheroes one. The Brother character has great room for expansion, and I want to see what I can do with him before the 2nd preview on Saturday. Whether I can replace much of the very good Xmas material by then I don't know. Let us see.

Saturday, 24 February 2018
Rastamouse & Krazy Kat - a week of comics from Northumberland

Have I spent more times in schools this year than at this time in any previous year? Feels like it*. (Says he, going off to Google, or possibly Bing, to find out if it's true). This week saw me doing four days in schools in Northumberland, courtesy of Gil Pugh and the Hexham Book Festival, beginning with a day divided between Seaton Sluice and Seaton Delavel. Here you see the covers of the comics we produced together, my having added the colour after the fact.

In Alnwick, where my day was split between Duchess and Glendale schools (you might spot the name of one of those schools inspiring a Stranglers quote on the cover) their suggestion for titles (chosen by everyone in the class coming up with a name, and us playing a knockout game to choose the favourite) gave me the chance to draw Bananaman for the first time in ages, and Rastamouse for quite poossibly the first time ever.

I've been there twice now, and neglected every time to ask why Dr Thomlinson's school is so called. Sounds like the name you'd give to a venerable public school, but it's simply a rural middle school in Rothbury. Simple as it is, I love how the cover of Shpoke came out when I coloured it (the character was taken straight from the drawing by one of the kids, Kacie I believe was her name).

Tweedmouth, rounding off the week, gave me the chance to slip in a bit of comics history for them. Hands up who recognises Krazy Kat and Ignatz Mouse? Well, you know them now.

The celebrities these eight groups chose to star in my demonstration strip were Donald Trump (only twice this week), Declan Donnelly (also twice), Gordon Ramsay, Harry Styles, Anthony Joshua (I had to google him, a boxer apparently), and most original of the week Barry Scott from the Cillit Bang ads.

*Yes. Yes I have. So far this year I've posted 6 updates of comics from schools, effectively making 6 weeks worth of school visits. This time last year I'd posted 2, this time 2016 I'd posted 5, this time 2015 it was 4, and in 2014 it was 2.)

The Socks appearing on BBC Radio Leicester this morning. Not a bad interview we must say.

Superheroes 2nd Preview Leicester Feb 24 2018

Our second ever preview for the new Superheroes show went down very well at The Kayal at Leicester Comedy Festival, and I think I've come to a clear conclusion - the Christmas material has to go.

It was another excellent show, a sellout as far as I can tell, with a higher proportion of Socks fans in the audience than last week (about 50% had seen us before), so a very good test of the material. And, though the only direct feedback I have so far as from Hev, Mum and Diana Stevens, who were all there, I'm pretty sure that there's one criticism that most viewers would have - where were the

Superheroes?

The biggest changes since last week's first preview were:

- New Audience-In music (Holding Out For A Hero, which need re-recording because the music drowns the vocals out)

- New song Steed & Mrs Peel, which is too long, but parts are funny

- I'd already dropped some Christmas stuff, so we had no Christmas Carol at the end, and no Fannying Around The Christmas Tree. I also staggered Smell Like Xmas, so we only got the first line of it at the start of the show, then the complete song at the end.

But, with 60% less Christmas, there still seemed to be too high a ratio of Christmas to Superhero material.

The fourth and biggest change was that I'd built up the part of The Brother, and that was really promising. I'd written too many Rhyming Slang pieces for him - three in the show are funny, 6 are not. But when it looked like The Brother was likely to usurp the

Sock on the right, when the Sock on the right returned he got a sympathetic aah from the crowd. We also got pantomime boos for The Brother when he returned. That's all working very well in the structure of the show.

Last night's performance was let down by messy changeovers, which meant some parts weren't made clear. Cross Channel Superman, for example, made no sense because it wasn't set up properly.

So, notes for the next stage of writing are:

Smell Like Xmas - and the whole Xmas storyline - has to go
Wonder Woman - now good (with full spin) but needs costume change added

Joker teeth - very good, but needs Batman story around it expanded

Motion Capture - badly set up so no-one seemed to get it

Nursery Rhymes - lose this

Peter Parker - still good, but could be relegated to Audience In music

Brother scene 1 - lose one rhyming Slang, keep it tighter

Racist Brother Song - good, but we're straying from Superheroes by now

Horror Song - good, but not Superheroes. Need something like this but on topic

Little Baby Jesus - good but we could use something better

Steed and Mrs Peel - good but too long, & again not Superheroes. Needs Avengers after

Superman part 1 (Jor El) - not funny enough

Superman part 2 (glasses) - excellent. Hooray, the show has 15 seconds that are perfect.

Dead Ringer - very good. But we need Superman story to end satisfactorily here

Brother scene 2 - good. Is this the best place for it? Interrupts flow, just when we were getting stuck into Superheroes

Cross Channel Superman - a bit of a mess because it was set up badly (didn't segue well from Brother scene). Would prefer strong new sketch here.

Split up - messy

Brother scene 3 - messy

All By Myself - messy but getting there

Finale - at this point we're all set for a finale, so I'd better write one. In preview 1 we did Christmas Carol, which was very funny but not the right thing. This week we did Smell Like Xmas, which was very good, but not satisfactory because it's not Superheroes.

The bottom line is we need good, complete Superheroes sketches - our "plays within plays" as Hev calls them - and we need to replace the Christmas material, and the weak parts, with them. Hev & I came up with a great Ant Man routine in the car last night, so we're getting it together. The good thing is that the structure of the show works, and that the new character of The Brother plays well with audiences and can do more in the storyline if he's used well.

Next stop, March's previews in Glasgow and Bath. By which time we'll see what's become of our Kickstarter campaign. it has a few days to run, and you can join in with it here: https://tinyurl.com/soxkick18

Wednesday, 28 February 2018
Weather Maps & musicals - a
month's random Facebook posts

BBC WEATHER MAP

Feb 9: Hooray! After years of me
(and no doubt many others)
moaning about it, the BBC has
corrected their weather map. The
country is now the right shape
again - and green! - after a decade
of being beige and tilted so that
London looked gigantic and
Scotland looked tiny. One can only
assume a Scot or a Northerner has
got into a position of influence at
BBC News or the Met Office. Either
way, well done at last BBC.

Feb 5: **Teenage Rampage - The
Chinnichap Musical.**

You know when you have a brilliant
idea that you know you're never
going to have time to write. Here's
today's. A jukebox musical based
on the songs of Nicky Chinn &
Mike Chapman. A teenage Romeo
& Juliet (only they're called Mickey
and Alice) set in the 1970s with
gangs of skinheads vs normal kids
at a comprehensive school in the
Midlands. You're welcome. Songs
include:
Teenage Rampage, Hellraiser,

Blockbuster, Ballroom Blitz (Sweet)
Mickey (Toni Basil)
Living Next Door To Alice, I'll Meet
You At Midnight (Smokie)
Tiger Feet, The Secrets That You
Keep, Dynamite, Lonely This
Christmas (Mud)
She's In Love With You, Devil Gate
Drive (Suzi Quatro)
Better Be Good To Me (Tina
Turner)
Kiss You All Over (Exile)

Cue someone telling me this has
already been done and it was a
total flop

Yes! Rude Puppets are headlining
this year's Obscure City Nickname
Comedy Festival!
(Also taking actual booking for
Edinburgh Previews, right now. No
city too obscure!)

Feb 5: Last night I had a dream that I'd seen spoilers from the new series of Doctor Who. Emilia Fox was being interviewed on a chat show about her part in the new series and they showed clips. Fox played a green-faced lady who lived in an aztec like ruin in a jungle. In each of the three clips we saw the face of a distinctive male villain with a moustache, which we saw printed on an old clay coin and somewhere else. Then in the final clip, a CGI spaceship or machine assembles itself atop Emilia Fox's jungle temple in the style of a Transformer, and we see that when it's complete it form the face of the moustachioed villain. Oh and it

sounded like Rose Tyler was there, but it could have been someone who sounded like her.

Has anyone else dreamt a spoiler for a show or movie that's not come out yet?

Feb 23: Has anyone seen a good **Netflix original movie**?

One would be forgiven for getting the impression Netflix only makes bad films. We've watched a few stinkers now - Ricky Gervais' Foreign Correspondents, Bill Murray's Very Murray Christmas, Mascots (gave up 15 mins in), Okja (I deeply disliked), Beasts Of No Nation (so miserable we couldn't watch it to the end), and more. Added to which they've taken over the onerous task of green-lighting Adam Sandler movies, suggesting Netflix really is the new Direct-To-Video. Now they've become the box they buried Duncan Jones in. I will concede Mudbound was good if schmaltzy.

Anyone seen a Netflix movie that wasn't the sort of thing you'd catch on a plane or a waste of your eyes?

Feb 20: Are we going to get the first ever Doctor Who title

Mute review – Duncan Jones's sci-fi thriller is a Netflix disaster

The Moon director has delivered a catastrophically misjudged riff on Blade Runner with an astoundingly dull performance from Alexander Skårsgard

THEGUARDIAN.COM

sequence to feature the screen filling with lager? It's my dream come true - Beer & Doctor Who!

Feb 1: Watching this **Top Of The Pops** from Jan 1985 was a stark reminder of one of the big things that was lost when they stopped putting pop music on mainstream telly: black faces on TV. In this particular episode, every single act in the studio is predominantly black (inc Smiley Culture, Amii Stewart, Grandmaster Melle Mel, and an obscure soul act called The Limit).

And, though it's not ideal to only be represented by musicians, it's undeniable that the loss of Top Of The Pops (and the other pop music shows across the other channels) decimated the number of BAME faces on British telly.

NB, I do think most things, in this regard, are better now than they were 33 years ago.

Feb 10: You know when you have a dumb idea you know you'll never have time to write? Here's today's - **Laptops**. A Romeo & Juliet story involving the little creatures who live inside our laptops and make them work (we all know they're there). One day a Mac falls in love with a PC... you can write the rest of the film yourself. (Remember where you heard it first)

Feb 24: Don't know whether to feel informed or tainted. Purely by chance I learned a new word. And it's offensive. Would anyone else have known, without looking it up, who or what an **Octoroon** was?

Feb 23: **Bing sings and Walt disnae.**

That didn't take long. Ten minutes ago I was gnashing my teeth finding that Google Image Search no longer works, and now I've discovered Bing Image Search. Turns out it's got functions that Google never had. From being the joke search engine that people use in TV shows, it's now my bookmarked search engine of choice.

What'll I discover next? Alta Vista?

Friday, 2 March 2018
Fat Cows & Overweight Pigs -
more comics by kids

A theme emerged in the comics produced by pupils at Olveston Primary in Gloucestershire, with portly farm animals being their subject of choice. And why not. From there, in the face of a supposed "Beast From The East", that is to say a threatened cold weather front, I drove from Gloucestershire to Ilford to stay overnight and watch snow fall on my car.

As it happened the snow amounted to nothing, and so I did my day of classes at John Bramston Primary in Hainault and made it home safely. Two comics by 4H, and a talk to the whole school in assembly? Easy peasy lemon squeezy.

Wednesday afternoon's drive to Manchester went surprisingly well, though the snow was starting to fall quite seriously. Then, very luckily for me, the day at Manchester Academy ended early, at 1.30, so Hev & I were able to hit the road home two hours earlier than expected. It looks likely that, had we left those two hours later, we would have got stuck in the snow. The following morning's news was full of drivers on the M5 near Taunton who'd been stuck in their cars overnight. So, phew, and no more travelling needed till next week.

The celebrities these five groups chose to appear in my demonstration strip were Tom Jones, The Pope, Michael Jackson, Declan Donnelly and, most original of the week, author of Diary Of A Wimpy Kid Jeff Kinney.

Fri 2 March 2018

Edinburgh Fringe on sale already

The Socks' new show, Superheroes, is on sale already. In fact it went on sale on March 1st. I've never had the show on sale so early, a full five months before our run starts on August 1st.

And by the end of today we've already sold 10 tickets. I'm looking forward to drawing my sales graph, but to be honest it feels a little bit premature. And that'll be a long tail at the start.

But with sales starting, and a day in the office (during which I was hoping to rewrite the entire show after last weekend's previews but failed to write a thing), I did manage to produce a few new

versions of the Socks as Superheroes, and a half dozen adverts to tweet over the coming months. Here's another one, since you asked so nicely.

Oh yes, I'll have to make a banner ad won't I? That'll be next.

Scottish Falsetto Sock Puppet Theatre: Superheroes at the Gilded Balloon, Edinburgh Fringe August 1st to 26th 2018 - ON SALE NOW.

Gilded Balloon Box Office
Fringe Box Office

Saturday, 3 March 2018

Scammed and snowed - Facebook posts of late

Phew, that was close. Just had my credit card scammed and, thanks to Santander, spotted it in time. Someone had tried to make ten £100 payments from my credit card this morning. Santander texted me, I rang em back, and now I get a new card in a week. Seems they'd cloned my card. So now I'm looking back to see where that could have happened. Hotel in Alnwick? Morpeth? Berwick? Wisbech? Ilford? Oh god, I'm a credit card scammer's dream, aren't ?

Here are the payments they'd tried to take by the time I got on the phone to Santander. A day later I find they'd kept on trying, and got even bolder this time:

I mean good luck trying to get two grand out of any of my credit cards! I do hope they catch these scammers. I don't want to cast aspersions without any foundation, but there is one of the hotels I stayed at last week that now makes me think it was the kind of place where it could have happened. I won't name it, in case I'm wrong. (But I've mentioned them to Santander, just in case).

Blimey we were lucky. Hev & I

Thursday, 8 March 2018
Stupid Man Smashes Face In The Concrete - comics by kids

This week's schools took me from Manchester to Birmingham to Monmouth, and ran the gamut of school types, from inner-city school to posh girls school. At Blakesley Hall Primary in Birmingham I've done my thing of trying to represent the demographic of my pupils on the covers, and they've reciprocated by coming up with probably my favourite title of the week.

At Alma Park in Manchester the kids' choice of title gave me the opportunity to parrot the logo of a Marvel comic from my childhood. I haven't googled to see what the Thing's actual logo looked like, but I bet it's exactly like the one I've done*.

Actually this is probably my joint favourite title of the week. They came up with another corker at Haberdashers Girls School in Monmouth. And what did I say about going from inner city to posh? One of my schools this week had a few of those traits that come from being a bit under-pressure: school gates that are locked when I

travelled back from Manchester to Clevedon yesterday afternoon and got home just as the snow was building up. In fact our road was already un-drivable-up when we arrived. Now we're watching the TV news with people who've been stuck on the M5 overnight. So, phew. Big thanks to Manchester Academy for ending the day two hours early.
Here's what Clevedon looked like yesterday. The beach covered in snow, not something you usually see in these parts.

Wooa-oh we're halfway there, wooa-oh living on a prayer...Thanks to today's new pledges, the Socks Kickstarer campaign for Edinburgh Fringe 2018 is now halfway there, with 10 days to spare. Well done everyone. Keep spreading the word and we can do it. (Right now we need less than 45p from all the followers of this page and we've done it!)
https://tinyurl.com/soxkick18

need to get in, to stop parents from using it as a drop-off zone; a photocopier where you have to bring your own paper (someone thinks that's a saving, rather than just inconvenient and frustrating); a staff room with no tea bags for guests, etc.

Then you get to Haberdashers in Monmouth and you know you're in a posh school when the teachers eat the school dinners - which today had the option of veg lasagne, veg chilli & tacos, fish and chips, and a fourth main dish, and a fully stocked salad bar, and... well you get the picture. Old girls of the school include the Official Harpist to HRH The Prince of Wales, don't cha know.

The celebrities these six groups chose to appear in my demonstration strip were JK Rowling, David Bowie, Selena Gomez, Simon Cowell, Michael Jackson and The Queen.

* Not bad. Pretty close. Preeeeeeeety close.

Tuesday, 13 March 2018
Snow and schools - photos from my travels

It's been a busy start to the year with Comic Art Masterclasses in schools, coupled with writing and previewing the Socks' new show Superheroes, and doing art jobs for the Chartered Insurance Institute and finishing off my Bible Society work. Busy busy. But never too busy to put on a good pose for my ID badge at a school.

When you're working on a show about Superheroes, you start seeing them everywhere. This mural was on a boarded up shop in Weston Super Mare.

The scalding cup. You could market this thing as guaranteed to scald. It was one of those schools

who take Health and Safety precautions and really run with them. In this instance, and you get this in quite a few schools, they've fixated on the ban on taking hot drinks into classrooms. The argument, quite reasonably, is that kids might get burned by your cup of coffee (and the school will get sued, which is most likely the real cause for concern). Their solution, however, is anything but. Their solution is the scalding cup. I was brought a cup of tea in this lidded flask, which was very kind, and for which I'm very grateful. But I couldn't drink it.

As soon as I took a sip from the narrow lip at the top I had to spit it out as it was scalding. So I sealed it back up and left it. Whenever I returned to it, it was still undrinkably scalding hot. Of course it was - it's a vacuum flask! That drink will never get any cooler. Ergo it will never be drinkable.

Double ergo, it is consequently scaldingly hotter and more damaging to any child than if I'd taken a normal self-cooling cup of tea into the classroom. A normal cup of tea, of course, would have been drunk in a couple of minutes, thus eradicating the danger to the kids, whereas this high-temperature time-bomb remained blisteringly deadly until the end of the lesson. I finally poured it into a cup in the staffroom, left it to cool a minute, and drank it. But really.

If you ever wanted a definition of Health And Safety done very badly, this is it.

I don't usually take photographs of my food, but I thought this was worth a snap. Bringing to mind John Finniemore's excellent song Put It On A Plate, we have my breakfast at Cheadle House Hotel brought to me in a jam jar. Very nice, sweetly stylish. In fact I liked the hotel so much I stayed there again a week later. But this second

time I did without the breakfast. At £15 a pop, and with Heather joining me for the second visit, that's a bit steep for some beans in a jam jar.

Having done caricatures at a Holiday Inn in Wakefield, Hev and I stayed over in town and the following day were able to take in the Hepworth Gallery, which is one of the country's finest fine art galleries. This fun installation was by Anthony McCall and is the perfect thing for entertaining families and non-art-lovers, and attracting a wider audience to the gallery, without letting the side down. It's a smart conceptual and installation artist who can straddle the divide between challenging brain-doodles and theme park ride. If you haven't been to the Hepworth, you really should.

My travels included journeys around the country in the face of the Beast From The East, a day or two of cold weather which we'll be

struggling to recall when it comes to Big Fat Quiz Of The Year time. It did, however, give the opportunity for some nifty pictures. This is the view from my hire car during my trip to Berwick On Tweed.

When you're writing a show about Superheroes, you start to see them everywhere. This was a shop window in Stratford On Avon (visited en route back from Leicester).

Friday, 16 March 2018
Glasgow Previews - a tale of two audiences

A Sock with Lobey Dosser and Rank Bajin, outside Dram in Glasgow

The two previews in a row the Scottish Falsetto Sock Puppet Theatre have just done in Glasgow (of our new show Superheroes), playing at our regular venue Dram! as part of Glasgow Comedy Festival, have been quite the education.

Following on from the first two previews in Leicester in February, I'd done an extensive bit of rewriting, removing all the Christmas material, and introducing lots of brand new all-Superhero stuff. Now I had a Wednesday night and a Thursday night show in which to test out whether what I'd written was funny and worked, with a whole day inbetween to make improvements.

The first night, Wednesday, was a joy. It's a small venue, so the 30 punters we had made as much noise as a sellout, and responded beautifully to most of the show. It was clear that some pieces needed work, so I spent Thursday trimming the chaff, writing new gags, changing the order, and essentially sharpening up our act.

Then came the second night, with the same size of crowd, a much better script (I thought) and a response from the audience that bordered on the funereal. Right from the start they were hard to get a laugh out of, and there was an element I could hear (and, of course, I can't see them) who seemed downright hostile. At the end I had loads of people coming up to me telling me how much they'd enjoyed the show, and a couple of people explaining that there was one table - a group booking of ten, so effectively a third of the audience - who were distracted and on their phones all the time (someone referred to them as Hooray Henries) and they seemed to have spread a bad vibe around the room stopping everyone else from enjoying themselves. Who knows? I recorded both nights but haven't brought myself to watch the second night yet. I certainly came away with the resolve to make the show so solid and funny from the start that it would win over even the most reluctant audience.

(I am guilty, I think, of becoming complacent, and over-used to audiences with a high percentage of Sock fans. Though our magic usually works on any audience, I am wrong to take for granted their being on our side from the start. When I can "feel" that there are people not "getting" the Socks, not buying into their word play and their silliness - and, if what I've been told is correct, not even paying attention to the show, which would make everything they do pretty nonsensical and inevitably not funny - then it bounces back on me. When a crowd is "going" with it, every laugh they give provokes more from us, until you can surf the wave of laughter, your only worry being too long a gap between them. This was the experience on night one. On night two, I was more surfing the silences. And when a gag is met with silence, you convince yourself it's not funny, despite the evidence of the previous audiences who'd reacted like it was the most hilarious thing they'd ever heard. It's a funny old business).

Here's what we gave them and how they reacted. This is the running order for Night Two. Between Wednesday and Thursday we'd lost the Nursery Rhymes routine.

Opening lines - Ken Dodd and Steven Hawking gags. Mild response night 1, silence night 2. **Batman, Robin & Flash** gags - Night 1: a hit. Night 2: a couple of groans.
I'm A Sock - Night 1: Perfection, got all audience on side. Night 2:

Winning some over

Cosmopolitan routine - Night 1: Very good, built to great laughs (would have put it on Youtube, but want to keep it in the show, very strong opener). Night 2: They were not finding this funny.
Ang Lee & Bob Kane - new gags for Night 2. Some laughs.

Motion Capture - Night 1: Good, best reception yet, Night 2 (with good new prop) some response
Peter Parker Song - 1: OK. 2: Thought I could hear some people leaving during it.

Faraday, Boron, Sagan gags - 1: Excellent, 2: OK
Brother scene 1 - Night 1: Fantastic, lots of adlibs, audience loved it. Night 2: Some laughs from the people who were trying hard to enjoy the show. I could feel one side of the room were liking it.
Your Racist Brother song - 1: Great, 2: OK, some laughs, even from the tough element

New Batman lines for Night 2 - some laughs
Batman and Joker - 1: Hilarious, 2: some good laughs

Steed & Peel - 1: Good but slight drop from laugh level. 2: No laugh level to drop from.
Brex Men - 1: OK but needs better punchlines, 2: About the same (booing for the politicians)
X Men Scottish - 1: Good laughs, but last line flopped, 2: Some laughs, last line got a groan

Avengers Reel - 1: Lots of good laughs esp Hulk verse, 2: Not quite so good but not bad
Wonder Woman - 1: Flop (but by night 2 standards pretty good), 2: Awful

Fantastic Four - 1: Good laughs, nice applause at end. 2: Surprising laughs, but silence at end.
Brother scene 2 - 1: He came on to pantomime boos, which was great, and Sock On The Right was getting "aah"s. Great laughs. 2: Some laughs, but table to the left audibly restless

Schrodinger gag - Night 1: Whatever. Night 2: A new Sock fan, sat in the front row, started at about this point in the show to start SAYING THE PUNCHLINES JUST BEFORE I DID! How that was supposed to help anyone I don't know. He went on to do it a few times. The Socks tried to get some banter out of this, but frankly it was doing more harm than good, and by now I'd acknowledged the odd mood of the room, which is often a bad thing to do cos, unless you're turning it around, that can just make it worse.

DeGrasse Tyson gag - Night 1: Genius. Night 2: Ignored. I think the audience were waiting for guy in the front row to work out the punchline and say it first

Superman - Night 1: An absolute joy. Getting laughs for the Jor El Kal El schtick, which wasn't working in Leicester, this piece just built and built, until we got to the Glasses routine, by which time we were surfing comedy waves of laughter. Night 2: A struggle, but I was getting there, and keeping them, until the buggers started groaning at the farmyard bit, then I won them back with the Glasses but it was so disappointing to have lost them when it felt like they could be coming back.

Dead Ringer song - good both nights. It's almost as if we know how to do this if you'll give us the chance.

Harley & Ivy's Cookery & Gardening - good both nights, though struggling a bit the second night

Brother scene 3 -Night 1: Okay, but overlong and lacking laughs. Night 2: Script tightened well, but hard to tell because of the nature of the night

What I've Learned speech - new for Night 2, and actually went well. Because it's more dramatic than comic, it grabbed them, then got laughs for its punchlines. Very promising.

All By Myself - Night 1: Good but messy, Night 2: Better, and good response

Finale Avengers - Night 1: Lots of laughs, but messy. Night 2: Better performance, good laughs, but chummie in the front row leapt in from the start, doing the "Irn Bru" punchline just before me, then guessing the next punchline wrong, neither of which was helping. Whole piece tailed off with rewritten end. So we need a better climax, otherwise it's a good last bit.

To prove it's not my imagination, here are clips to compare and contrast. The same gags and how differently they went down on nights one and two. No, you're obsessing about it!

At which point we told them, both

nights, it was the end of the show. On Night 1 they interrupted their applause to sigh good-naturedly, and we rewarded them with **Smell Like Xmas**. On Night 2 the end fizzled, and when we said we'd reward them with a song, some bright spark on "that table" responded with "Oh god no".

We got good laughs by attacking him, and the song went well. But god that was a hard show, and no matter how many people come up to you at the end and say how much they enjoyed it, I defy any comic to come away from a show where the audience didn't laugh as much as you think they should, feeling good about it all.

Interesting to compare this year's Glasgow Previews experience with our 2015 Brighton Previews experience, as documented here, where Minging Detectives had two distinctly different receptions too.

Roll on Bath Comedy Festival the week after next, when they'll be getting the whole shebang - with even more improvements than we just did - and we'll be able to hear how an audience is supposed to sound again (fingers crossed).

Sunday, 18 March 2018
Socks In Space - The Full Show

As part of de-cluttering my laptop, and backing things up, I've put the whole of Socks In Space up on Youtube, so do please enjoy it.

It's a single camera recording of the 2014 Leicester Comedy Festival performance, from the start of the spring tour, the show having been our 2013 Edinburgh Fringe show. So it's not the greatest quality recording, but you'll find lots of it great fun. With the usual caveat that, to get the full experience, you really had to be there.

The running order is

I'm A Sock song
SF genre gags leading to Bottle routine
Comics to movie gags
The Comics Song

The Avengers routine
Improv routine
War Of Worlds gags
Doctor Who / Capaldi routine
Green Screen Song
Alien routine
Andy Warhol song
Fireball XL5 song
Countdown routine
Star Trek routine
Chekov routine
David Bowie song
Ding Dong routine
Star Wars finale

The recording ends before we get
to Star Wars I'm afraid.

Meanwhile over at the Sitcom
Trials....

Because it has its own blog, I rarely
mention **the Sitcom Trials** here in
my blog, and to be honest there's
not been much to say for the past
year, not since the end of the 2016
So You Think You Write Funny
season which culminated in
Edinburgh that August.

But Friday morning, when I was
waking up in Glasgow and
recovering from a rather dispiriting
preview gig (and reading the
comment on the blog from one of
the audience members I'd not been
happy with, turns out the feeling
was mutual), I got a helpful
Facebook message showing me
that someone was using my name.
Namely RTE in Ireland launching
what they rather cheekily called

"The First Sitcom Trials."

Needless to say I wasn't crazy about this, and sent a few messages by a few different mediums, letting them know that the name was taken, and hoping they weren't trying to pretend to be us. They replied nicely:

Hi guys, just came across your tweets this morning. We would like to assure you that we are not using the same name as you. Before we start anything we also do a name check and make sure no one else is using the same name. We are going by "Radio Sitcom Trials' and you have 'The Sitcom Trials' so different names and didn't need to ask permission. We do see how it isn't the 'first ever', this was more directed as the first in Ireland, as it's only Irish born or Irish residents that can enter. To clear this up I will retitle it the 'first ever Irish'. Sorry for the mix up and hopefully that answers any questions. If you would like to get in touch about anything my email is M.......e. Have a lovely weekend, Michaella.

So I'm happily tweeting support for them and plugging their contest, since it can't do the Sitcom Trials brand any harm. Plus, I've been told, you can't copyright a name. And as long as they're not using my actual format, they're free to call their show what they like.

The deadline for entries is March 31st, and the details are here.

Scottish Falsetto Sock Puppet Theatre

Real name: Kev + Sutherland

Created by comedian and comic book creator Kev F Sutherland in 2005

TOUR GIG DATES   REVIEWS   NEWS

Upcoming Dates

Scottish Falsetto Sock Puppet Theatre: Superheroes
Date: Wed 1 Aug 2018
Venue: Gilded Balloon
Price: £8 or tickets are available
Show starts: 22:00

BOOK NOW

Wednesday, 21 March 2018
"Festival stalwarts" - Chortle

Chortle is the most respected authority on comedy in this country, so it's incredibly pleasing when one gets a good mention. In the story today plugging the Gilded Balloon's Edinburgh tickets going on sale, they've put us prominently in the article as "festival stalwarts". It may only be a small thing to you, but to move from also-rans to stalwarts is a definite pleasure.

Added to this, they've listed our full Edinburgh run on their gig guide, which is a boon and a boost. So, many thanks Chortle. We look forward to delivering a show that merits a review in August.

Here's that article in full.

Gilded Balloon floats its first Fringe shows of 2018

Luisa Omielan, Zoe Lyons and Rhod Gilbert

Luisa Omielan, Zoe Lyons and Rhod Gilbert are to play the Gilded Balloon at this year's Fringe.

The comics were announced in the venue's first batch of programming today.

Omielan will be headlining Gilded Balloon's biggest space, the Debating Hall, with her new hour, Politics for Bitches. She said: 'I believe it's my right to have an opinion on something I know absolutely nothing about.'

Gilbert continues his return to stand-up six years after his last tour with some more "work-in-very-very-early-progress' shows. He said: The world's gone totally mad since I last toured in 2012, and my head's all over the shop. It's time to get back up there sort it out once and for all!"

Lyons will be presenting her new show Entry Level Human, while other perforemrs include Robin Ince in the Museum of Scotland, Melbourne Fringe Best Comedy award-winners The Travelling Sisters, 2017 So You Think You're Funny? Maisie Adam with her debut show Vague and festival stalwarts The Noise Next Door, Notflix and the Scottish Falsetto Sock Puppet Theatre.

Also in the programme are Laura Lexx, Justin Moorhouse, Alison Spittle, Stuart Mitchell, Patrick Monahan, Fred Cooke, Red Richardson and Scott Gibson.
Published: *21 Mar 2018*

Monday, 26 March 2018
Chubby The Space Cow - comics by kids

A return to Prema Arts in Uley in Gloucestershire looked in danger of being snowed off (a bit of a theme this year) but went ahead fine, with two classes going beautifully, and a lovely cover in the form of Chubby The Space Cow. And I was on a door split, which I should do more often (memo to self).

Then, in a contrast to my last visit to Dublin where I was there for a whole week, this was a whistle-stop one-day visit to Larkin school, which I haven't been to since 2010. A sambo is what they call a sandwich, honest. Though beware what happens when you tweet it, is all I can say.

Whizz Kidz Manchester was a short one-off class with the wheelchair kids, some of which I've worked with before, in Birmingham, most of which are new to me. And I'll be working with another group again soon, in Liverpool next time. There was no access to a photocopier, so this group went away without a finished printed comic, but I still coloured the

components up after the fact, as is my wont.

The celebrities these five groups chose for my demonstration strip were Elvis Presley, David Beckham, The Queen, John Cena and Donald Trump.

Friday, 30 March 2018
Metro & Lovehoney - Socks
Preview in Bath

Check the Socks out all over the centre pages of Metro newspaper, at the start of Easter weekend and on the day of their Superheroes Preview at Bath Comedy Festival.

Lucky old Bath Comedy Festival, courtesy of good old Nick Steel its

OUT OF YOUR MIND Running for the next fortnight, this great event sees a completely different, brand new play performed each night. They'll all be conceived, written and performed by local children and adults from the age of five upwards. A great way to get any budding writers and thespians in your family inspired. Thursday until April 8. The Egg Theatre. Prices from. theeggonbryael.org.uk

SCOTTISH FALSETTO SOCK PUPPET THEATRE
They're daft, hilarious, and for over 12's only. Just this show will definitely have them - and the adults - in stitches. Thursday, Widcombe Social Club, Bath. bathcomedy.com

A DAY AT A TIME...

Plan the first Easter week with our bumper diary planner of events the kids will love, says **Chantelle Horton**

sterling organiser, had the privilege of a 90 minute show for this our tenth appearance at the Festival. (We are, if you're interested, the only act to have played all ten festivals.) They were also the first of this year's preview shows to have the actual title (Superheroes) in the programme. Leicester, Glasgow, and Brighton in May put their programmes together so far in advance that we've been listed only as "The New Show", cos I had no idea what the theme of the show was going to be back in November. In fact Nick had us supplying him with info so close to the deadline that we even managed to squeeze onto the front cover of the Bath programme:

So, how about the show itself? Thanks for asking, it was brilliant. Our best Superheroes Preview yet.

And, with the exception of the last show at Glasgow, they've all been pretty good.

Because of the odd nature of the audience at our last show, the 2nd Glasgow Preview, which I'd spent a day rewriting and preparing, I didn't feel that rewrite had had a fair test, so tonight in Bath they got that rewrite with no changes (just two removals: the then-topical Ken Dodd and Stephen Hawking gags, and the lame Wonder Woman routine).

In addition, because we were doing a 90 minute show, the Bath crowd, which was about the size of the Leicester audiences and very appreciative from the start, got a 30 minute warm up from the Socks, doing our old favourite stuff. Luckily for us, though we've been there 9

times before, alternating between shows at Widcombe Social Club and the Rondo Theatre, they've been seeing the new show every time, so last night most people hadn't seen our 'staples', so gave a smashing reception to the Halloween, Michael Jackson, and Magic routines, and to Walk On The Wild Side and Sweary Poppins. And there was another addition to our comedy arsenal - Lovehoney.

Lovehoney, whose banner ad you can probably make out in the background of this Sock selfie, are new sponsors of the festival, and they do sex toys. Which gave us the opportunity for some great ad libbing, and nice callbacks throughout the show. Sadly I only videod the second half of the show, the Superheroes bit, so didn't record most of the Lovehoney adlib

material, so you'll have to take my word for it that we were on form.

Thus warmed up, the Bath crowd were the perfect test for the Superhero materialwhich is holding up very well, and will be developing further by the time of its next preview in Brighton in May (if anyone has any preview opportunities in April, we'd jump at them). High points include Superman and the Racist Brother story; improvements are needed to the Avengers Reel, the Avengers skit, and the X Men; a lot needs to be done to integrate or give better punchlines to Batman, Harley & Ivy, and the Fantastic Four; and items that may hit the cutting room floor include Steed and Mrs Peel and Spider-Man, if and when better material comes along. The writing process continues.

Saturday, 7 April 2018

Alan to Chucky - new comics by kids

Aha! It's the Easter holidays, so this week's Comic Art Masterclasses have been in some unusual extra-scholastic settings. The above pair of comics were produced with kids in the Swansgate shopping centre in Wellingborough. I'm pretty sure the kid who wrote the title "Alan" on a bit of paper, and ended up having it chosen as the group's favourite, didn't have this particular Alan in mind. (In fact I suspect he was trying to write, and misspelled, the word Alien).

On Friday I did Easter holiday classes in Chingford and Walthamstow, both of which had a slight impromptu nature about them, with kids wandering in and out. Regardless of which we managed to produce a couple of good looking comics. I was particularly pleased with Spiderball Vs Chucky once I got home and coloured it up.

Another pair of comics from the Swansgate in Wellingborough. We were very lucky in having access to the photocopier, which meant I was able to send all the kids away with their A5 comic containing a strip by every one of them, and all of their caricatures.

Given the chance, that is if I arrive early enough in the day, I like the draw a flipchart to leave them with. Some of these find a good home in the schools I visit, and occasionally, when they've not found a more deserving claimant, a lucky kid gets to take one home. One of the above from Wellingborough is now in a child's collection somewhere.

The celebrities these six groups chose to appear in my demonstration strip were Simon Cowell, Kevin Hart, Michael Jackson (twice), Donald Trump, and The Queen.

Friday, 13 April 2018
Avengers Reel - new from the Socks

Brand new from the Socks, the Avengers Reel. Enjoy.

It's a song that's been in the last three previews (Glasgow and Bath) and may stay in the show with a bit of a rewrite. Or it might hit the cutting room floor and end up being part of the audience-in music, we're at that stage of development at the moment.

What's that you say? You want to read all the words? Oh go on then since you asked so nicely...

AVENGERS REEL

Summon The Hulk, Black Widow & Ant Man, Iron Man and Hawkeye Captain America, Thor & Nick Fury – he's only got one eye Get em on board the Helicarrier – it floats up in the sky The Agents Of Shield are waiting to greet you, then we'll beat Loki

You talk to Iron Man, and I'll talk to Loki,
And I'll talk to Captain America About how come the women don't get fillums of their own

So they wait to hear Avengers Assemble

Avengers Assemble tada tada
With Rober-ut Downey Juni-ah
And Scarlet Johanssen uh huh uh huh
And Mark Ruffalo with his shirt off

Samuel L Jackson plays this bloke with a patch on
He's Nick Fury the super techno spy
Meanwhile Thor is a Viking who's much more to your liking
Also Hawkeye's here, but we don't know why

You'll get a romance and a bromance
Then some fighting in 3D
You'll always get some in jokes
And a cameo by Stan Lee
Marvel universe movies
Are all made by Dis-a-nee

And they all have a scene at the end when you are going

There is a Solder, a Winter Soldier
We bring him into things, though he's not interesting
He is quite plucky, his name is Bucky,
And no-one here has heard of him

There's a wee man here and his name is Bruce
And he wouldnae say boo to a goose
Make him angry he's big as a hoose
But the Hulk won't rip his troosers
  Let the wind blow slow, let the wind blow fast,
But it won't blow up his incredible ass
His shirt and his socks they may not last
But the Hulk won't rip his troosers

Sequels abound like a rash on your bum
With these Marvel franchises
If you don't like the last one there's lots more to come / And also TV series
   Punisher, Daredevil, Jessica Jones,
Luke Cage and Iron Fist
And the Inhumans and the Defenders
And several more that we've missed

So
If it wisnae fer the Avengers where would you be
You'd be watching superheroes made by DC
Though Wonder Woman wisnae bad the rest you neednae see
Cos you know you can trust the Avengers

Saturday, 14 April 2018
Devil Who Farted Rainbows - new comics by kids

We haven't had Donald Trump title suggested by the kids in my Comic Art Masterclasses for a while, so this one from the library in Potters Bar was a treat to draw. It's the second week of the Easter hols, so these classes were once more extra-scholasticular (if it's not a word, it should be).

My second day of holiday classes in Walthamstow and Chingford was fun, made all the more entertaining by me having, first, to pick up a flipchart pad in the town centre before the first class. Then I had to zoom from a school in Walthamstow to a school in Chingford. Not a long journey but, as I realised when I punched it into satnav, one that was going to take me all of lunchtime. I had, you see, pre-programmed the postcodes for my destination into satnav in advance, to save time. So when it came to heading for Chingford, I simply hit the pre-installed postcode (which appears in "history" as a pre-visited address) and off I went. Don't worry I didn't get caught out by accidentally going back to the town centre where I'd been earlier to buy a

flipchart, I skipped that.

It was only when I was a good few miles up the Chingford Road and starting to turn into the M25 that I realised I'd skipped an address too far. Instead of going to Chingford, I was going back to Potters Bar, where I'd been two days earlier. Long story short, I arrived 20 minutes late, but the class was excellent. Phew.

I'm doing a series of classes with CLAPA - the Cleft Lip and Palate Association - and couldn't avoid the obvious pun, on the flipchart above. Sue me.

The celebrities these five groups chose to appear in my demonstration strip were Kim Jong Un, Roald Dahl, Michael Jackson, Donald Trump and, most original suggestion for a while, Gilbert O'Sullivan (chosen because one of the kids' Dads is a friend of Gilbert, or Ray as they know him, and stay with him in his house in Jersey).

"I do love a nursery rhyme. Cock robin? No it's just the way I'm standing."

Scottish Falsetto Sock Puppet Theatre

Sunday, 15 April 2018
Socks Win Best Joke Award!

Wow! Well here's a pleasant surprise. The Scottish Falsetto Sock Puppet Thetre just won Bath Comedy Festival's inaugural Lovehoney Innuendo Best Joke Award. Here's us, with special guests Donald Trump and The Queen, and our award which is shaped like... well, it looks like the Christmas trees from The Louvre to us. (Thanks to Louisa Gummer for the photo)

Lovehoney have been the major sponsors of this year's Bath Comedy Festival, and the Socks' got some great laughs by managing to keep them going as a running gag during their Edinburgh Preview last week. Which is probably what impressed them

enough to make our gag the winner. They wanted a gag with innuendo in and, let's be honest, it's not our greatest joke ever. But it gets a laugh and, much more importantly, it just won us a flipping prize! Shaped like a butt plug.

I say shaped like. I'm reliably informed that it is in fact an actual butt plug from Lovehoney's factory, painted gold. Blimey. All I can say is, if you've got the trots that bad, you're going to be better off with Immodium. (Which is just the sort of gag I wish I'd thought of on the podium when I picked up the trophy at the end of Saturday night's Gala show, rather than just delivering my winning gag very badly, as myself rather than as a Sock).

Donald Trump, in the photo above,

My wife didn't like my new coat.
So I said, ▓▓▓▓▓▓▓
"Yes, but as long as I wear this, I'll never get wet!"
And she replied, ▓▓▓▓▓▓▓
"Yes, and as long as you wear that, neither will I..."

Drew Tayl

"I'm so bad at oral sex, it'll blow your socks off."

Nick Doody

is played by the brilliant Lewis Macleod, who I found myself working with for the first time since 1998 when he was part of the cast of my BBC Radio Theatre studio audience pilot Meanwhile, co-starring Ronnie Ancona and Geoff McGivern. There, names succesfully dropped. The Queen is played by one of the theatre company Rare Species, who seem to do sterling work all over the country.

So, what was this joke of ours? Brace yourselves...

"I love nursery rhymes"
"Cock Robin?"
"No, it's just the way I'm standing"

The winner, ladies and gentlemen, of the inaugural Bath Comedy Festival Lovehoney Innuendo Joke Award.

The runners up came from a pretty illustrious list of contenders: Nick Doody, Christian Talbot, Drew Taylor, David Luck, Konstantin Kisin, Iona Fortune and Drew Taylor. Here are my two favourite runners up...

Thanks again Bath Comedy Festival and Lovehoney, the award takes pride of place in our trophy cabinet alongside... the sides of our trophy cabinet. Next stop the Edinburgh Fringe's Best Joke Award (unless, of course, that's already been decided).

Cracking pair win innuendo prize

Socks clean up

Two sock puppets have won an award for the best innuendo at the Bath comedy festival.

The Scottish Falsetto Sock Puppet Theatre – the creation of comic Kev Sutherland – won the accolade for the exchange: 'Ooh, I do love a nursery rhyme' 'Cock Robin?' 'No, it's just the man I'm standing'.

News: Scottish Falsetto Sock Puppet Theatre Wins Joke Award
By Bruce Dessau on 15/4/2018

The Scottish Falsetto Sock Puppet Theatre has won the inaugural Lovehoney Innuendo Best Joke Award at the Bath Comedy Festival.

They are pictured here with their award - or maybe it's Donald Trump and the Queen? No, it's the Scottish Falsetto Sock Puppet Theatre.

Here is the joke that won it for them:

"Do you know what? I love nursery rhymes?" "Cock Robin?" "No, it's just the way I'm standing."

They are previewing their latest show Superheroes, which they will be taking to the Edinburgh Fringe, in London on April 27 at the Canvas Cafe, 5 Hanbury Street, E1 after Juliette Burton's Happy Hour. More info here.

Tags: Falsetto

Sunday, 15 April 2018

Cracking pair win innuendo prize - Chortle

Lovely coverage of our award win on Chortle.

Cracking pair win innuendo prize

Socks clean up

Two sock puppets have won an award for the best innuendo at the Bath comedy festival.

The Scottish Falsetto Sock Puppet Theatre – the creation of comic Kev Sutherland – won the accolade for the exchange: 'Ooh, I do love a nursery rhyme' 'Cock Robin?' 'No, it's just the way I'm standing'.

Their award was presented by Lovehoney, the online sex toy shop that sponsors the festival.

Here's a video of the joke:

Published: *15 Apr 2018*

Sunday, 15 April 2018

Award coverage on Beyond The Joke

More nice coverage, this time on Bruce Dessau's Beyond The Joke.

The Scottish Falsetto Sock Puppet Theatre has won the inaugural Lovehoney Innuendo Best Joke Award at the Bath Comedy Festival.

They are pictured here with their award - or maybe it's Donald Trump and the Queen? No, it's the Scottish Falsetto Sock Puppet Theatre.

Here is the joke that won it for them:

"Do you know what? I love nursery rhymes?" "Cock Robin?" "No, it's just the way I'm standing."

They are previewing their latest show Superheroes, which they will be taking to the Edinburgh Fringe, in London on April 27 at the Canvas Cafe in Hanbury Street, E1 after Juliette Burton's Happy Hour. More info here.

2

Monday, 23 April 2018
Dandelion Experiment
Urgh, look away. Not for the squeamish. I have undergone, not for the first time, The Dandelion Experiment, by which I endeavour to rid myself of a wart, by application of Dandelion juice. You can see from the grisly photos above that it is, to a degree, worked. But what a gruesome degree. The blistered and pussy stage you see in figure 5 was how my face looked for two days in schools. In all the process took about 7 days to clear. fig 1 is before and fig 2 shows the application of dandelion juice, on Monday April 16th. By Tuesday it had darkened for fig 3, then by Wednesday it was starting to swell and blister. Fig 4 shows it as its worst, as it was around Thursday and Friday, and fig 5 shows it the following Monday, all cleared up. There is still a small wart there, but not quite as visible as it was to begin with. And the second smaller wart that was threatening to form above it has, I think receded. I could apply a second treatment but, I fear, I have too few days when I can hide away from the public. (I applied it on a Monday, knowing I didn't have a school till Thursday and thinking it would be

Tuesday, 17 April 2018
Book Of Ruth all coloured
It's taken me a while, in between other work, but I've finally got The Book Of Ruth"s 12 pages coloured. Now I just need to colour Rahab and I've got a whole book good to go. I do hope it's going to go somewhere soon.

gone by then.) So ends this month's medical experiment. I hope it adds to the greater weight of knowledge.

And, knowing nobody will be reading this...
PS - A cunning ruse of suspicious type includes clues
Lovely. Opportunities come my way frequently, but I don't always take them. Often I let them slip through my fingers. Knowing whether they're worth taking can be the problem. I, for example, have been invited to do Britain's Got Talent twice. Just imagine if I did it? Ultimately I did one audition and failed it. Saying that, I then got asked about doing America's Got Talent. To be honest, it was only an exploratory phone call. Brutally honestly, they didn't want me. Retrospectively, I'm just guessing at that. Or, of course, they might have wanted me, but they needed me to prove that. Knowing that to be the case, I should have pressured them more. Except I didn't really want to do it. And it's not as if I'd have won.
Now another opportunity has come along, and I've said yes. Not that you'll know about it for months because it's top secret. Did you know that when you're involved

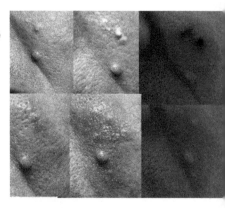

with a project like this you have to sign something? A Non Disclosure Agreement. Forms sent by email that need printing and signing and scanning and resending. Right pains in the arse they are. Of course I signed them, and returned them, and then I learned what I was to be involved in. My oh my, this will be fun, I hope. The truth be told, though, you probably won't even see me on the screen. Highly likely all you'll see will be my hand and the back of my head, for a couple of seconds. Even then I most likely won't speak.
And, though I'll be using my comic drawing skills, you might not be impressed. Possibly you will be, I shall try to do my best. Pressure of time, though, will most likely work against that. Regretfully I'm not getting paid much.
Eventually I'll be able to talk about

it, and it'll be a good anecdote to have. Not that that'll be happening till at least October, possibly November. Then the cat will be out of the bag, and you'll all go "was that it?" Is that your big secret, you'll say. Can no-one keep a secret these days? Evidently I can't.

Demented Donkey Fights The Environment - comics by kids

A busy weekend of Comic Art Masterclasses, taking me from Milton Keynes to Sutton Coldfield, to Liverpool, and back to Milton Keynes, included a couple of days where I was trying to get the kids to tailor their strips to the theme of the environment, climate change, and the like. Here were the covers created with the pupils of Longmeadow in Milton Keynes. Because these are going to be printed in a colour magazine in the summer, I was pleased with how they came out, drawn in the class on the day and coloured when I got home.

Despite the obvious ecological theme, these two were in fact from Dyson Perrins school in Malvern and had nothing to do with the MK eco project. That's a character from Pokemon, apparently. Like I'd know. And, yes I agree, radishes do not lend themselves to a good cover design.

The comic on the left was made with the smallest group of the week, just 5 teenagers at the YMCA centre in Sutton Coldfield. I'll be going back to work with larger groups in the coming weeks. Then we see the comic from Hazeley school in Milton Keynes, where I was so keen to draw a local landmark, then got hamstrung by the fact that no MK landmark is really all that photogenic. That's a place called The Point, now you ask.

In Birkinhead I worked with the Whizz-Kids again, a group of kids with a variety of abilities, some on wheels and some not. They produced some cracking work. And to the right you can see the flipchart I did for the YMCA class.

This is what you get when I arrive an hour before the class starts.

The celebrities these groups chose for my demonstration strip were Ariana Grande, Donald Trump, Paul Walker, Ant McPartlin, Lionel Messi and David Attenborough. (With the group in Hazeley I dispensed with the demo strip and, guess what, it made no difference to the quality of their work.)

Tuesday, 24 April 2018
Parket? Radio sitcom joke cock up

Badly Done Joke Alert!

If you listen to the trailer for Radio 2's Funny Fortnight (on this iPlayer clip 10 mins in) you'll hear a gag that's not only unoriginal (of which more shortly) but also absolutely buggered up.

From new sitcom The Taylors, the exchange goes:
"That old flooring, what's it called?"
"Parquet?"
"It was, but it's much warmer now we've got the carpet down"

Now I know it's an old gag because I used it in my BBC radio sitcom pilot Meanwhile, recorded in the self same Radio Theatre in 1998. But that's not the worst crime. The worst crime is the delivery.

The joke works because "parquet" sounds like "parky", an old-fashioned word for cold. But in this clip, the actor pronounces the word "par-ket". Which renders the whole gag meaningless.

How someone could have let that slip into the recorded sitcom without noticing it - then used it IN THE TRAILER! - defies description and beggars belief.

If I'm so clever, why aren't I writing a new sitcom on BBC Radio you ask? Probably because I post bitter and twisted things like this. Even I wouldn't want to work with me.

Parket. Kids today.

Tuesday, 24 April 2018
Fighting The Superhero Way

A new song and video from the Socks, Fighting The Superhero Way. If it's lucky, this will be part of the audience-in music for Superheroes, so you'll only be subjected if you come and see the show live. Which you will be doing, won't you?

Monday, 30 April 2018
Jack Kirby Song

Brand new from The Socks (edited in my hotel room in Switzerland while working at Aiglon school, now you ask), is a musical tribute to Jack Kirby. Intended to be part of the audience-in music for the new show, Superheroes, it might not even make it that far. But it was fun to write, I hope you enjoy it.

Thursday, 26 April 2018
My Top 10 Influential Comicbooks

Folks are doing this, so why not. 10 comics that influenced me.

1 - Terrific
Before this I'd read Playhour & Robin and Pippin & Tog, but when Terrific (and its sister paper Fantastic) started reprinting Marvel strips I suddenly started paying attention to comics. I remember vividly a three panel sequence by Steve Ditko where The Hulk emerged from a hole or a tank (which I can't find online, so I've probably Maconied it). This was when I first 'got' comic strips. I was five years old.

2 - Asterix
Four Asterix books came free with Total petrol*. Though I've been

aware of that fact for nearly 50 years, I've not till now asked the question: where on earth was there a Total petrol garage? I've never seen one. Whatever, four Asterix books came free, the rest you had to pay for. To be honest, their content may ultimately be better than any other comic I go on to mention in the rest of this list. (Update: I've looked at the rest of the list, Asterix is the best of the stuff on the whole list. Sorry rest of the list.)
*Asterix The Legionary, Asterix The Gladiator, Asterix & The Big Fight, and Asterix & Cleopatra.

3 - Lion & Thunder
A series of amalgamations, using the British "Hatch, Match, Dispatch" publishing tradition, meant that I ended up reading comics by default. Terrific had been swallowed by Fantastic, which then became Smash & Pow Incorporating Fanastic. And just as I was getting into the revamped Smash, with its Eric Bradbury lead strip and Leo Baxendale centrespread, it was sucked into Valiant & Smash. I'd started reading a new comic called Thunder and, within 6 months, found myself reading Lion & Thunder which, with such strips as Geoff Campion's Spellbinder alongside Adam Eterno and Robot Archie, was such a delight I totally failed to notice the Marvel reprint strips had long since disappeared.

4 - Planet Of The Apes
Marvel came back into my life when I discovered the reprint strips based on my favourite TV show, Planet Of The Apes. I quickly discovered Marvel UK were producing about 10 comics a week, reprinting 40 pages of comic strips

in black and white in every issue, meaning my generation was able to mainline every classic Marvel strip, from the early 60s superheroes through to the latest creations at a rate of over 300 pages a week. And you got change from a quid. The black and white litho printing of art from everyone from Neal Adams to Barry Smith, Gil Kane to Jim Steranko, enabled British readers to see the pages bigger, and clearer, than our American cousins had endured a few years earlier, buried in blotchy colours. This affected and nurtured a generation of comic artists who were about to flourish.

5 - Look-In

The highest quality printed comic art in the world at the time, by my reckoning. (As you can see from these copies in my collection, I treated them with scant respect, using them to decorate my diary). Though the stories only came in two-page instalments, the art by John Burns, Martin Asbury, Harry North & Mike Noble on such adaptations as The Tomorrow People, The 6 Million Dollar Man, Doctor In Charge and Black Beauty were devastating and put all other contemporary comic art to shame. Marvel art at the time looked so shoddy in comparison it convinced me that someday they'd be so desperate they'd even employ me.

6 - 2000AD

To begin with I dismissed 2000AD for not being as well written as the Marvel reprints, and new colour Marvel comics we were starting to be able to get (in particular Howard The Duck, which remains my favourite series of the period). But I

got hooked when Starlord comic came out and, just like had happened in my earlier childhood, got subsumed into 2000AD. Early favourite were Dredd and Robo Hunter, with Bolland and Gibson being fan favourites. Then came Alan Moore and a proper revolution in comic book writing took place. See also Warrior.

7 - The Spirit

The longest delay between a comic coming out and me discovering it has got to be the forty years that passed between Will Eisner's Spirit appearing in American Sunday newspapers, and my starting to read it when it was reprinted by Kitchen Sink Press in the 80s. These strips, especially Eisner's artwork and storytelling, were as impressive then as they must have been when they first appeared. As I

had the pleasure of saying when I gave a speech introducing Will at the 2003 Raptus Comic Festival in Bergen, I had for years attributed to lesser later copyists most of the techniques that Eisner had in fact originated. If my comic strips have draw on/ borrowed from one person more than any other, it's Will Eisner. (Also Doonesbury, I "do" Doonesbury so much!)

8 - Swamp Thing

That period in the early eighties, when American comics started using British talent, was something so momentous it's hard to describe to a younger generation used to an international publishing world. Just 10 years later I was to find myself working for Marvel, but in 1983 that was beyond our comprehension. DC and Marvel were so distant, so unreachable. And the fact that our

own Alan Moore was then writing comics that made his American contemporaries look so primitive, derivative, old fashioned, it really was something to experience live. The post-modern approach to comics, whereby writers will "do an Alan Moore" and revive an old or rather silly character by bringing it into a gritty realistic world or deconstructing and remaking it, has become the norm, leading to the Christopher Nolan Batman films and the DC and Marvel Cinematic Universes, of which we're no doubt going to tire soon. 35 years ago, on a typewriter in Northampton, is where that glorious nonsense started.

9 - Viz

Somewhere in a parallel universe, a guy called Chris who had no pretensions to being a comics creator and little or no interest in the world of comics started writing and drawing some nonsense that, quite possibly to his surprise, lots of people liked. Within a decade it became the biggest selling comics magazine in Britain, probably the world, and 40 years on it's still going. Viz remains possibly the only comic book that has genuinely made me laugh out loud (though Giles and Doonesbury are personal favourites, and make me smile, they've never made me spit a drink like Viz).

10 - Beano

I never read The Beano as a kid, having discovered Marvel reprints when I was five. But in 1999 I somehow noticed they were running long-form stories by writer-artist Mike Pearse and that they were excellent. The best storytelling I had ever seen in the Beano. I endeavoured to follow in his wake and, thanks to visionary editor Euan Kerr, found myself being able to write and draw a number of serialised comic adventures in the Beano, for a good few years, which remain the work of which I am proudest. Mike Pearse's work remains my favourite work I have ever seen in that comic, though the work of a recent generation including Gary Northfield and Nigel Auchterlounie has been of a similar high standard. I have my fingers crossed for its continued survival.

Saturday, 28 April 2018
Superheroes 6th Preview - London
April 27

Thanks to Juliette Burton, who gave us a slot after her Happy Hour show at the Canvas Cafe just off Brick Lane, the Socks were able to do an extra Preview of **Superheroes**, ahead of May's shows in Brighton, and following on from March's Bath show (which in turn followed 2 nights in Glasgow and 2 in Leicester). This was an invaluable preview, getting me back up to speed with what needs improving, while letting me test out the material I've written this month.

The audience, only about 15 strong but lovely, had already watched an almost 3 hour show featuring Juliette and three other comedians (Rik Carranza, Lorna Shaw, and

Lost Voice Guy), being the surviving hardcore of a larger crowd, staying on after 10.30 on a Friday night. The Socks eventually started at just short of 11pm. They were what I'd call 'An Edinburgh crowd', being above-average comedy-savvy, younger and more cosmopolitan, so a very good testing ground. Here's what we gave them and how it went.

Opening gags - Wayne/Robin/ Flash. Good. Opening with quickfire gags is a good start.
Opening gags continued - Awards (new). However, continuing with 7 more puns, no matter how good (and I'm pleased with this batch) isn't so good. It sets the show up as a night of puns and is not the best way of building their engagement. These should appear later in the show and even be scattered through it.

I'm A Sock song - The usual test of a new audience (only 1 of whom had seen the Socks before). They laughed in all the right places and we had them.

Cosmopolitan - Excellent.
Bob Kane gag - Good. One isolated arcane pun works fine.
Motion Capture - Brilliant. Delivery a bit messy, but the core gag works. Ending needs improving.

Ang Lee / Ditko gag (new) - Good. Two puns together work fine
Comedy Award / Nursery Rhyme gag - Good (excuses the gag).
Spiderman Song - Now seems a bit weak. Should replace this.
Plot / Maguffin gags (new) - Brilliant, and make the structure clear

Science Faraday/Sagan - Shortened by one gag, v good
Hulk gag (new) - First groan of the night, but good

Brother 1 - Excellent. Fewer prop laughs, all from the lines & characters
Your Racist Brother Song - V good, good laughs throughout

Batman - V good. New gag okay. Teeth - brilliant.
Urine/Nuts/Crazy gags (new) - Very good

Crossover inc callback (new) - Good. Needs to be called back later
Steed & Mrs Peel Song - Another weak song. I think I'm the only person who likes it, it'll have to go.

Avengers (moved) - Excellent. Much better in the middle of the show than as a finale.
Avengers Reel - Needs improving. (Failed to re-record it since Bath, will be better when shortened and keys changed)

Fantastic Four Appeal - V good, laughs in the right places (Needs callback later)
Brother 2 - Excellent. Good laughs from lines again, not so much from props
Shroedinger/ Tyson gags - Okay but spoil the flow slightly

Superman - Origin gag (new) v good.
Jor El/Kal El to The **Kents** - Excellent. First time an audience has properly gone with this routine. Need callback later.
Glasses - Not as many prop laughs as before, but that's fine as the lines funny
Dead Ringer Song - Excellent
Harley & Ivy - Messy start so audience puzzled for first half, then laughing for the rest.

Daredevil (new) - Very good, brilliant laughs for the new prop. Punchline disappointing.

Brother 3 - Very good.

If I've Learned speech - good
All By Myself - Very good, but need to perfect those prop changes

And we ended the show there, which was doubly fortuitous. Firstly, because I haven't written the finale properly (though it has a handful of new gags that didn't get tried), and also because the show was over-running and, unbeknownst to anyone, we had to get out of the venue by midnight or we'd get fined. So me finishing after, I think, 55 minutes was perfect.

So, in conclusion, and in advance of Brighton: I now have a good story structure that holds it together and enables me to lose and insert material. We have lots of great one-liners, but need:

Replacement for Spider-man song,

ideally with a strong routine
Replacement for Steed & Mrs Peel,
again with a strong routine
Reduced and re-recorded
Avengers Reel
Proper Finale (with callbacks to the
running jokes set up already)
Tightened up props (especially
Brother, whose mouth is not so
funny it can be allowed to never
work properly)
... and anything that tackles the
many superheroes that haven't had
a look in to the show yet. Wonder
Woman and the X Men, for
example (Brexit Men hit the cutting
room floor this time round).

Onwards and upwards. Next stop
Brighton Fringe, May 26 & 27.
Book now.

Tuesday, 1 May 2018
Fred Astaire & Chief Wiggum -
comics by kids in Switzerland

I was delighted this week to get the
chance to return to the Swiss Alps.
In fact I liked it so much, I'm going
back again in a fortnight. All thanks
to Authors Abroad who, this time,
arranged a two day visit to Aiglon
College, which is in Villars Sur
Ollon in Switzerland, the same
village where you'll find Beau
Soleil, the school I visited three
years ago, and whence I'll be
returning later this month. Here are
the comics produced by two groups
of Year 8s. Fred Astaire wasn't
their idea, that was my indulgence.

My second day at Aiglon saw me
working with years 4 through 7, and
here are their various productions.
The college looked after me
marvellously, feeding me three
times a day if I needed it, to the
highest standard. I think the prize
for Best School Meals ever has
been won, if only by the desserts
made by their pastry chef. It puts
crumble & custard in the shade.

The previous week I journeyed to
North Kent College in Dartford,
where I worked with one group all
day, all college aged. This is a fun
variation on my usual routine of
working with mostly primary school

kids, giving me the chance to up my game, do something more than the same old same old, and work with students who, in some cases, can draw better than me.

Here's an example of some of the stuff I did on the flipchart with the North Kent students. The left hand page shows me helping them break down their stories. I'm chuffed with myself when I can help them in this way. With younger groups, either they don't understand what I'm talking about when we get on to montages, different angles, and more sophisticated techniques, or maybe there's just not enough time. Here, clearly, there was. Oh, and that's a drawing of a dinosaur, for reasons I can't now remember.

The celebrities these five groups chose to appear in my legendary demonstration strip were Vladimir Putin, Eddie Redmayne, Gigi Hadid (I'm told she's a model, m'lud), David Beckham, and Pablo Escobar.

Sunday, 6 May 2018
London, Switzerland, Lake District - Travels With My Art

So where were we? If it was last Friday, then I must have come to the end of a week when I'd visited schools in Milton Keynes, Sutton Coldfield, Birkinhead, Milton Keynes again, then Dartford in Kent, and on Friday night I was off to Brick Lane to do a Socks preview gig, setting off home at midnight and getting to bed at 3 in the morning.

Which means Sunday was the start of the proper travelling. Sunday morning (April 29 now you're asking) I flew to Geneva, and from there took the train ride to Villars Sur Ollon for two days of classes at Aiglon College. This is the same alpine ski-ing village I'd visited a

couple of years ago, working at a different school to which I'll be returning later this month. This time the weather was good so I got some marvellous views of some rather impressive alps which, of course, look like nothing at all when you try and photograph them.

The school days were lovely, textbook, with Aiglon taking the prize for Best School Dinners ever. When the fish and chips includes a pea puree instead of mushy peas, and desserts are the work of a five star pastry chef, you realise you're in a place where the words "wasted on kids" have no real meaning. Annual fees are 111,000 Swiss Francs, or £82,000. Once more I come home realising I could have charged more.

No sooner had I got back home

(after a flight that was supposed to go at nine o'clock and ended up setting off some time after eleven, frustratingly short of the three hour mark after which they have to pay you compensation) than it was time to set off on my travels again, this time to the Lake District. I knew I was to do a school there on Friday, paid for by DC Thomson who had given me as a prize in a Beano competition. When I worked out it was going to be a 6 hour drive to get there, I realised I was going to have to use up all of the day before to get there in time.

Therefore it was the most fortuitous stroke of luck when Authors Abroad, the lovely people who'd just taken me to Switzerland, rang up asking if I could do another school in the Lake District. So it was that, at one day's notice, I did a bonus half day at Arlecdon Primary near Cockermouth.

Hev and I set off at 6 in the morning, getting to Cockermouth for midday, and I did a half day at the school (they only have 34 pupils, so half a day was all they needed), and we stayed over. The next day, as planned, I did the full day at Beckstone Primary near Workington, and then it was off on

another long drive. A swift and uninterrupted 5 hour drive to Milton Keynes which, given that this was the Friday before a Bank Holiday, and a sunny Bank Holiday at that, was quite remarkable.

After a night at the Holiday Inn in MK, which is becoming a bit of second home, this is the 3rd or 4th time we've stayed there, it was the 90 minute drive to London for a Top Secret assignment. I've actually signed a Non Disclosure Agreement about the job I did, which involved quite a few hours of sitting around chatting with my fellow Beano creator Nigel Auchterlounie, after which the two of us did something which involved drawing a couple of comic pages which will be appearing in some form or other later in the year. I look forward to filling you in on all

the details sometime in October or November. In the meantime, here's a sneak peek.

I shudder to think how many miles I've driven in the last fortnight. But, for the record, here's my list of destinations from the past month:

Wellingborough, Milton Keynes, Chingford, Potters Bar, Walthamstow, Cleobury Mortimer in Shropshire, Malvern, Milton Keynes again, Sutton Coldfield, Birkinhead, Milton Keynes yet again, Dartford, Brick Lane London, Geneva & Villars Sur Ollon Switzerland, Cockermouth, Workington, Fleet Street London and home.

Next week I take it easy with a school in, would you believe, Clevedon. Then, of course, it's the Isle of Wight, then Switzerland again, but let's think about that when we have to, eh?

Sunday, 6 May 2018
10 Favourite Albums

Since I know no-one can possibly care about my Top 10 favourite albums (yeah, like I've looked at all ten of any of yours) I'll get this over and done with in one go. Ten fave albums, in no particular order. You may care to play Top 10 Albums Bingo with this list. If more than 2 of these albums are on your list, or even in your collection, I'll be amazed.

Well Well Said The Rocking Chair - Dean Friedman
It's hard to explain to kids today how much impact a comic-book loving humorous singer-songwriter can have on an impressionable teenager, but from his first single Ariel I was hooked. It's hardly as if he was singing about my life -

though picturing himself reading the Howard The Duck Treasury Edition on his album cover let me know we had a bit in common - but I loved the way he did it. Where some people see cheesiness, especially in his classic Lucky Stars, I saw humour, and an artist who was having fun playing with pop music, telling stories and breaking the mould. It was from this album that I learned the term S&M (no coincidence that, on his edition of Radio 1 Star Special in 1979 he chose Tom Lehrer's Smut), and heard for the first time the authentic sounds of a New York Deli (in The Deli Song, subtitled Corned Beef On Wry - do you see what he did there). I can still be found, in my car, knacking my voice trying to sing along to the bombastic closing track Don't you Ever Dare. And I couldn't give a good goddamn.

The Higher They Climb The Harder They Fall - David Cassidy

No one said this list was going to be cool. But anyone who thinks David Cassidy is the least cool part has never listened to this album. This concept album. Yes, you heard me. As David's pop star career went into a nosedive, he made this album about a pop star whose career has gone into a nosedive. The two minute drama in the middle, Massacre On Park Bench, is tragi comedy genius and shows that, though his mental health and self esteem were to decline a lot in the years that followed, at this point he had a good deal of perspective on who he was and what his painful career amounted to. I can recommend his autobiography Come On Get Happy if you want the backstory on the unhappy life of a teen idol, for

which this album provides a perfect soundtrack.

The Rutles - The Rutles

No Beatles in my list, just The Rutles. I bought this album on CD (in America in 1991, when it was as yet unavailable in the UK) long before I bought any Beatles CDs (in fact I only ever got round to getting Sgt Pepper). Neil Innes' songs sum up the Beatles' career, in many ways better than The Beatles. And they stand alone as singalong classics. When Oasis came along, I compared them unfavourably to The Rutles, and I think I still do. (For the record, The Rutles' movie has dated badly, but the music has got better with age).

Widescreen - Rupert Holmes

I'm proud to say I was a Rupert Holmes fan long before he started appearing on the Gilbert Gottfried podcasts and it turned out he's a fantastically witty and intelligent guy with an encyclopaedic knowledge of movies. On this movie-themed album he throws every idea, every orchestral twist, and probably some actual kitchen sinks into a set of songs that can be misconstrued as unintentionally funny - Letters That Cross In The Mail and Terminal having some gloriously cheesy storylines with terrible puns - until you realise he knows just how cheesy he's being, and he's loving it. I made a movie of Our National Pastime in my first year at art college, and I'm so glad I did. When everybody else starts becoming Rupert Holmes fans, I'll be able to point at that movie and prove I was there before all of you!

Flood - They Might Be Giants

Straying into territory some might call acceptable, even respectable, here's the album where I discovered the geeks' geeks, TMBG. They can do no wrong, and here's an hour of them doing not so.

Cosmic Thing - B52s

Oh, we're being far too popular again aren't we? But what can I say? There's not a bad track on this album, and if geeks are allowed to dance, then let them dance to The Deadbeat Club.

Tonic For The Troops - Boomtown Rats

The Boomtown Rats became unfashionable very quickly, and were soon outranked by the cooler spokesmen-for-a-generation like Paul Weller and Elvis Costello, and their fellow Dubliners U2. But for a brief time they were the smartest, and most successful, new wave act in town, and hits like Like Clockwork and Rat Trap knocked spots off all comers. Bob was also the best value for money pop star in a TV interview since The Beatles

- fact. The tracks on this album, though occasionally musically narrow in range, are nostalgic fun and still listenable. Ouch, damned with faint praise. But brilliant.

Day At The Races - Queen

It's hard to choose a favourite Queen album, cos they're far too popular and everybody else has heard of them, and you hear them all the time on the radio, and when that Freddie biopic finally comes out you won't be able to move for them. But for the duration of 7 albums (which, because it was the 70s, came out in less than 6 years) they were the greatest band on the planet, and can take responsibility for the musical part of my musical education. If there was anything done on a pop record that Queen didn't have a stab at doing better

than everyone else, I don't know what. I remember Elvis Costello mocking them on Radio 1's Round Table saying "Bryan May is to the guitar what Roy Castle is to the trumpet." Somehow he made that sound like a bad thing.

The Stranger - Billy Joel

Once again, I'm not sure why I felt middle aged Jewish singer songwriters from New York were saying so much about my life, but this record shares shelf space with the likes of Stephen Bishop, Janis Ian, and of course Dean Friedman. And I like it just the way it is. Scenes From An Italian Restaurant, isn't it? Jumpers for goalposts... (This is the record that pretty well tells the world how old you are. In 40 years time, possession of Ed Sheeran and Adele will do much the same thing).

Life - The Cardigans

They subsequently slagged their own album off as being an early work that sounded like old sixties songs. Which just goes to show you why you should never ask bands about their earlier, best, work. The best pop songs to come out of Sweden since Abba. And, since I've never owned an Abba album (he lies, he has Abba Gold, but the classic albums were only ever on loan from his sister), The Cardigans are in the chart, and always getting a replay. Rise and Shine everyone, I've finished my list, you may relax.

Monday, 7 May 2018
My Top 10 (ish) Favourite Films

Clearly I'm not a serious cinephile. I realise this from my Facebook friends who can quote entire movies, who go to the cinema almost daily, who see everything when it comes out rather than waiting till it's on TV for free, and for whom the movies are a much bigger deal than maybe they once were for me. But since people are indulging themselves with these Top 10s, who am I to buck the trend. These are 10 movies I've watched and rewatched, and will watch again. You are free to disagree.

10 Play It Again Sam (1972)
It may not be fashionable, or advisable, to include Woody Allen movies in your top ten these days.

What am I going to have next? A Bill Cosby movie and the collected works of Harvey Weinstein? But my movie education came through the works of Woody Allen, especially his "early funny ones". This movie isn't even directed by him, but it is his purest comedy stage play, and any comedy screenwriter who can deny being affected by Woody Allen's work is probably lying. If you want to argue, I'll be at Frozen Tundra 555-6535.

9 Sunset Boulevard (1950) /
Singing In The Rain (1952)
The history of Hollywood is punctuated by movies that celebrate the history of Hollywood and this pair of films, made when the movie studios were nearing their 50th birthday, nailed the genre from the start. Everyone knows this business is a joke. In Sunset

Boulevard it's a dark, gallows humour of nightmarish proportions, in Singing In The Rain it's a laugh and a romance. From The Player to La La Land, every movie about the movies is in the shadow of this pair.

8 Citizen Kane (1941)

More than any other film, Citizen Kane wears its ambition on its sleeve, with every shot crying out "look at me, someone!". It should, as a result, be an annoying endurance test, like watching a kid doing well at a spelling bee. Instead it's a joy, with Orson Welles' mischevious humour emerging through even the most straight-faced moments. Nowadays, when technical feats with cameras and technology are taken for granted, Citizen Kane still impresses with a dozen "how did they do that?" moments, coupled

with as many innovations that no-one had bothered to think of before, and an infinity of moments you've seen spoofed in subsequent movies & TV shows, by people who want to remind you that they too have seen Citizen Kane.

7 Young Frankenstein (1974) / The Man With Two Brains (1984)

As a reminder of how age affects us all, both Mel Brooks and Carl Reiner (still alive at time of writing, and both well into their nineties) have made the greatest comedies ever, and some stinkers. Comedy first, stinker later. Young Frankenstein is Brooks' best, MWTB Reiner's. Steve Martin, in turn, went from being the funniest person on the planet to Mr Schmalz, luckily leaving us with scripts and performances like this along the way. I'd have loved Robin

Williams to make it into one of my favourite movies but, I fear, no film has ever been as impressive as his stand-up.

6 An American Werewolf In London (1981)

Jon Landis really got lucky with American Werewolf. Because, to my eye, nothing else he made has been any good. Some might even call him a pretty poor film maker. But when he made this remake of The Wolfman, with a largely British cast, something about it worked magically. Also it's "Our Movie" for me and Hev, so there.

5 The Graduate (1967) / Tootsie (1983)

Mike Nichols and Elaine May, who were making comedy albums 50 years ago at the same time as Brooks & Reiner's 2000 Year Old Man, have had an often unacknowledged mark on cinema through their improvisation work. Though May's input on Tootise goes uncredited, her work was pivotal. And Dustin Hoffman has to be the benchmark for a non comedian doing comedy, which he achieves by hard work. Indeed he spoofs his own methodology, and his "asshole actor" personality, in Tootsie. It's in Graduate where you see this pay off. A timelessly funny and original film that almost every comedy since, from Bridesmaids to The Hangover via every Saturday Night Live starred movie, owes it all to.

4 Alien (1979)

Not every film on my list is a comedy, and here's an exception. Unless you appreciate the dark comic timing that's essential for a

good thriller or horror movie. As well as being a perfect thriller, Alien is a rare science fiction film in that it doesn't look dated. Ridley Scott created the dystopian future look that has remained ubiquitous in sci fi movies since, and is the main reason I never took to Star Wars. After you've been inside a grody spaceship like the Nostromo, how can you take spaceships with clean walls seriously again?

3 Reservoir Dogs (1992)

Again, most people don't think of this as a comedy, and it's true that it's not a laugh riot throughout. But Tarantino's reappropriation of the clean look of the 1970s, with the borrowing of a Hong Kong movie plot, and his total disregard for prevailing fashions, coupled with some out-of-the-box scripting and ingenious casting, made this a

movie so impressive it's hard to describe 25 years later. A decade later, we'd been so deluged by low budget heist movies that it was hard to do anything but blame Tarantino for starting it all off. But, as unoriginal movies go, this has to be the most original. Also, notably, the most recent movie on this old man's list of favourites.

2 This Is Spinal Tap (1983)

None more black. Too much perspective. You can't dust for vomit. We should record it in Dobly. Earth's most quoted movie remains one of its most delightful. The original mockumentary, merging improv with plot so skillfully it's possible to forget you're watching one and following the other, Spinal Tap became the model for most TV comedy of the 21st century, from The Office to Veep. Don't look for

it, it's not there any more.

1 Psycho (1960)

I have a feeling this was Hitchcock's favourite, it's certainly the one that he was proudest to call a comedy. And though I'm not in a hurry to watch horror, slasher, or shocking films, there's no denying this is the grandaddy of them all. It's so transcended its original small-scale made-TV-style roots, that it's almost hard to look at objectively. It's been remade as an art piece, in Gus Van Zandt's shot-for-shot remake and in Douglas Gordon's brilliant 24 Hour Psycho (which we've seen twice now, parts of that is, and could watch all day. Literally), and never ceases to impress. Like American Werewolf, a lot of its charm comes through luck as much as design, with assistant director Saul Bass and a TV crew working to a tight schedule coming up with results that possibly no one had fully in mind when they started. Some acting is dated, some green screen shots in cars are risible, and in so many ways it could be dismissed almost as a B movie. But everything comes together, with striking images, unprecedented twists (spoiler alert: don't look for Janet Leigh after the first 20 minutes), and not a second of screen time wasted, to give you very nearly the perfect use of 90 minutes of film. It's surely no coincidence that Mum went to see this movie when she was pregnant with me.

Tuesday, 8 May 2018
Avengers Infinity War

Will this make it into the show? Who knows. We might try it out in the previews in Brighton next week. Meantime please enjoy some of the fruits of our recent writing on Superheroes, our take on Avengers Infinity War.

Tuesday, 15 May 2018
Steed & Mrs Peel

A major item to hit the cutting room floor, here's the song Steed And Mrs Peel which I've just removed from the Socks new show Superheroes.

Riffing on the fact that there's The Avengers and then there's The Avengers, I thought this was quite a fun song, but I now think it's too off-topic to work. So congratulations to the punters of Leicester, Glasgow, Bath and

London, who are the only people to have seen this live. This recording comes from Glasgow in March.

The show is shaping up nicely, and it time of writing is preparing for its next previews in Brighton. See you all there.

Thursday, 17 May 2018
Yes, I Remember It Well - new song from the Socks

A new song, written and recorded while writing the Socks' new show Superheroes, and destined never to be in the live show, and probably not in the intro music either - Yes, I Remember It Well.

It's a song about the ret-conning, or retrospective writing of the continuity of a character, in a comic or movie. And, yes, I realise how niche that whole idea is, but I had to write it anyway. A little bit of audience research on Facebook established quickly that nobody understood all of the references in the song, and many people got none of them. The lyrics are below, if you want to make any sense of them.

Yes, I Remember It Well

(SPOKEN)
R Of course you know the Joker's origin? He was a stand up comedian, then he does a crime as The Red Hood and –
L No no no, he's called Jack Napier played by Jack Nicholson, and he shoots Batman's parents
R No Batman's parents were shot by Joe Chill. Yes, I remember it well.

(SUNG)
R Dick Grayson's Robin, that's no mistake
L No Robin's Jason Todd, and then Tim Drake
R   Ah yes, I remember it well

R And Wonder Woman is Zeus's kid
L Actually she's a statue, Hippolyta did
R Yes I remember it well

R Now Spider-Man, this I insist, Has webs that come straight from his wrist
L Actually they're from some wee wristbands
That he just sticks on his hands

R   For me to get all these things wrong
It's like they make it up as they go along
L Yes I remember it well

R Deadpool can't speak, I know I've seen
That fight with him in Wolverine
Yes, I remember it well

R   And Scarlet Witch is Magneto's
L then
She should be in the films with the X Men
R Yes, I remember it well

R The Mighty Thor's a bloke called Blake
L Turns out his whole backstory's fake
R It seems that happens quite a lot
It's like they retcon the plot

R It happens daily, or so it seems, Next thing you'll wake up, and it was all a dream

L And yes you'll remember it well

Wednesday, 9 May 2018
Dude Who I Don't Know's Name - new comics by kids

After a few weeks of travel, it was a treat to be invited to a school in Clevedon itself, All Saints Primary. The school's had a radical rebuilding and is a smashing shiny new building, with a semi-underground level, all very 21st century. And there are only two classes, so I was able to teach the whole school in a day. Captain

Clevedon made a contrived return in a comic whose title, Ganze Le Einsatz, was made up by a child taking random words from a German comic (Liga Deutsche Helden, which I brought back from Hannover early this year). It translates as Whole Le Insert.

In contrast to Clevedon, Beckstone is a six hour drive away, as recorded in my Travels blog, and a couple of delightful comic titles they came up with too. These classes were organised by DC Thomson, who awarded me as a prize in a school competition.

Arlecdon was the school who were also in the Lake District, and had me for a half day, thus helping out greatly with justifying the long journey up there. I love an homage when I get the chance so, apropos of nothing, they got the front cover of Action Comic No 1 parodied as their front cover. And a nifty flipchart too, including a Jim Steranko Hulk for good measure.

When I get a good half hour before classes start, it's good to get a flipchart drawn, to which I add once the kids are there. The drawing of myself is almost always done as part of the live class, as are any pictures that look that bit more rushed or scribbled. In the All Saints/Infinity War flipchart you can tell that Doctor Who, Wonder Woman and Spider-Man were drawn more on the hoof than the rest.

The celebrities these five groups chose to star in my demonstration strip were Dwayne Johnson, Cristiano Ronaldo, David Walliams, Simon Cowell (twice).

Deadpool - new from the Socks

A new routine and video from the Socks, their look at Deadpool. Do please enjoy. Will this make it into the preview shows that we're doing in Brighton this weekend? You'll have to come and see.

Tuesday, 29 May 2018
Black Panther - new from the Socks

New from the Scottish Falsetto Socks, and already dropped from the new show Superheroes, here's their take on Black Panther.

We tried this out in the live show and found there's nothing funny enough to do live in it, but it'll sit quite happily in the audience-in music before the show. So do please enjoy.

Thursday, 24 May 2018
Thor's Hammer Squashed My
Lunch - comics by kids

This bumper bundle of comics was
created by kids from the four
corners of the globe. Admittedly I
only travelled as far as Switzerland,
the Isle Of Wight, Milton Keynes
and Birmingham to meet them, but
that felt like far enough to be
getting along with. The above pair
were from my annual two-day visit
to Colmore Juniors in Kings Heath
where I do classes with all four
groups of their Year Fives.

The second batch from Colmore,
and a wonderfully eclectic range of
titles, comics strips inside. I never
show you those here on the blog,
do I? Well, for every cover you can
see, there are up to 30 individual
comic strips by pupils in there.
Count your blessings you don't
have to see some of them, but a
whole lot are works of genius. I
have quite the unique archive here
on my shelves.

This pair of beauties are the fruits
of my most recent journey to Beau
Soleil College, up in the alps in
Villars Sur Ollon in Switzerland. I
was there two weeks ago, visiting
the school down the road, Aiglon,

and here I was back again, at the
school whose annual fees are
€100,000. Yes, dear reader, this
time I did charge more.

This one comic from Shenley
Brook End is more by way of a
byproduct, from the ongoing work
I've been doing with a series of
schools in Milton Keynes which I'm
collecting up into an environment
themed comic for the Milton
Keynes Islamic Art and Culture
programme. On the right you can
see how, on the flipchart, I help the
pupils to visualise their story ideas.
To be honest, I don't get the
chance to do this often enough,
and it's most worth doing with the
most able pupils. Which is what I
was working with today. I had a
whole day with one group of year
12 and 13s and they did the best
work you've seen. It's going to look
good when it's printed (and given
away at Art In The Park in June).

This comic, and flipchart, came
from my class at the Hullabaloo
festival in Sandown on the Isle Of
Wight. I was there for two days,
spending the first day just drawing
caricatures and whipping up
interest in the class on the Sunday.
The flipchart was a result of that
extra amount of time on my hands,

I hope the kids appreciated it.

The celebrities these eight groups chose for my far-famed demonstration strip were Kim Jogn Un, Stephen Hawking, Beyonce, Barack Obama, Donald Trump, Prince Harry, Dan TDM, and most original of the year so far: Geoff Nutkins (he's an aviation artist who one of the kids has a jigsaw by, apparently).

Friday, 25 May 2018
"There's not another act like it anywhere" - Ken Bruce

"Scottish Falsetto Sock Puppet Theatre - there's not another act like it anywhere" - Ken Bruce

The Socks got a namecheck on the Ken Bruce show on Radio 2, courtesy of Socks fan x who emailed about our version of Earth Song. Hear the clip here.

Meanwhile that quote's going on the posters.

Monday, 28 May 2018
Superheroes Brighton Previews
May 26 & 27

In Brighton this weekend the Scottish Falsetto Socks presented their latest pair of previews of the new show, Superheroes, to a cracking response from two lovely crowds (at 3.45 and 5pm on Saturday and Sunday respectively, on two of the hottest days of the year so far, so many thanks to everyone who came). We had some very strong new material, and kept chopping out the weak stuff, all of which served to remind me that we still have to get the whole working together to make a perfect show.

Saturday's audience was about 50% Socks fans, and Sunday's was nearer 10%, meaning

Sunday's were a far more stringent test of what was genuinely funny material, as people who've never seen the Socks before really need won over and keep entertained, whereas fans let you glide by on charm and familiarity, and confidence that there's good stuff ahead.

All of which serves to make me extra critical of the material, but also confident that we're going in the right direction and that we already have some brilliant stuff in this show which, when it's completed, could be our best yet.

Between Saturday and Sunday I chopped the script up quite a bit - literally, I was using nail scissors and gaffer tape to do it. Below is the running order we ended up with on Sunday. Lost from the previous day's show had been the Awards gags (some nice puns riffing on the fact that we've won the Bath Comedy Festival Best Joke Award, but they don't fit and hold the action up), and the new Black Panther song (which will go into the pre-show music, and onto Youtube, but isn't funny enough for the live show). Also lost a callback to the Cosmopolitan routine which wasn't funny enough. Lost from the last preview, in London, was the Steed and Mrs Peel song.

SUPERHEROES RUNNING ORDER, Sunday May 27 2018
(All items good as before unless mentioned)

Opening Batman/Robin/Flash - just quick gags and straight into...
I'm A Sock song
Cosmopolitan routine / **Bob Kane Motion Capture**

routine - good. Needs better ending & integration with the rest.

NEW Hulk Ang Lee routine - good, should get better
Plot/ Maguffin / Cock Robin (this last gag only stays in the show cos it won a prize, and leads to...)
Spiderman song - this really must go. Working on song and routine to replace it.

Fantastic 4 appeal - good but needs integrating into plot, callback later
NEW Thanos / Who's On First - needs work

Science/Faraday/Sagan
Brother 1
Racist Brother Song
Batman/ Teeth / Urine/Nuts/Crazy - this now has a callback later but needs its storyline to be concluded

Superman / JorEl / Kents / Glasses
Dead Ringer song

Brother 2
Science gags
NEW Joker 2 - good, needs integrating
Harley & Ivy

Avengers
Avengers Reel - now re-recorded, with a verse removed, and the keys changed. Much better.
NEW Dr Strange / Wong / Thanos

Daredevil - only laughs coming from costume, need integrating into plot
Brother 3
What I've Learned

All By Myself song - too long, needs editing to half its length **NEW Finale** - good lines but needs to be a much more satisfying conclusion.

So we have a good plot structure (the superheroes unite to fight the supervillains), and we have possibly our first ever proper subplot (Racist Brother), but the whole hour needs to flow better, with all the characters' stories tying together in the finale. And it still needs a couple of zinger routines and songs that'll put it up there with our best shows. Hev & I busked ideas in the car on the way back from Brighton and already have some nice ideas for Wonder Woman, Catwoman and Supergirl that will be getting their first airing in Bristol on June 16th.

Keep watching Youtube for those outtakes and experiments.

To Infinity War parodies - and beyond!

Thursday, 31 May 2018
Isle of Wight to Switzerland - Travels with my art

In the last instalment of Travels With My Art, our intrepid adventurer had come back from schools in The Lake District to do a bit of Top Secret filming in London, about which we'll be able to tell you more in the Autumn (oh the excitement of signing an NDA, like it's the Official bleeding Secrets Act). Then the unexpected luxury of spending most of the week at my desk, writing more of the Superheroes show, making ads for it, and sending out press releases, before setting off on Friday for The Isle Of Wight.

In Sandown on the Isle Of Wight I had the pleasure of meeting, for the first time in thirty years, Paul McLaren, who had been the star sculptor at Exeter College Of Art & Design back in the day, and who still makes big machines, only this time they're oriented towards entertainment. He was one of the organisers of Hullabaloo, a two day festival as part of which I drew caricatures and did an art class. A much needed festival for Sundown, I would say as, off season as it is, it looks a little benighted and in need

of TLC. I'm sure in the summer it comes to life.

Wednesday saw me returning to Milton Keynes for the last in a sequence of visits, after which I then had to colour and assemble the pupils work to turn it into an 8 page magazine to be given away at Art In The Park in the summer. At time of writing, I'm waiting to hear what they think of the finished job (delivered at the end of the month).

Then it was back to Switzerland for a return visit to College Beau Soleil, which I last visited in 2015. These two days travelling for one day's work included the chance to take in the usual breathtaking scenery (in perfect weather throughout); to enjoy an art gallery opening with a bit of live jazz, all of which was very Home Counties in

feel, like going to a small gallery opening in Surrey, albeit one with a view of the alps out of the window; and to spend a grand evening putting the world to rights chatting with my new best mate Karl Nova. Karl is a performance poet and writer who was doing classes at the school, and is great company.

Two days at a school in Birmingham and three days at my desk later and we were off to Brighton for two Socks Previews, as detailed here. After which the return to my desk saw the start of the Superheroes comic (I broke the 24 page script down in front of the telly on Monday night and had 7 pages completed by mid week), and the writing & recording of 4 new songs for the show (Black Lightning, DC and Silver Surfer, which will all be part of the audience-in music, and Bechdel Test which will be part of the show,

for the next previews at least). That's what I call a productive few days.

The month ended with a party. Since I had a class in Guildford the next day, Hev came with me and we made an overnight stop in London so we could attend The List Edfest program launch party at Omeara, a club under a railway arch in Southwark. And very pleasant it wa too. A few comedy and cabaret acts made a good stab at being heard over the conversation, I saw a few familiar faces but had no chats longer than two sentences, and we picked up the new Edfest programme. A fun party, which we left early cos of work the next day.

I never said these travels with my art made entertaining reading, but it's nice to have a record of these things.

Thursday, 31 May 2018
Square videos?

And suddenly I've discovered how to make square videos, with a frame around them. God help the world there'll be no stopping me now. Having found out how to do it this morning (you use Keynote, which I find myself using for the first time ever) I've stuck our videos for Black Panther, Deadpool, and Infinity War into frames. Already the Black Panther one is on Twitter, the Deadpool one is on Facebook, and I have Infinity War waiting in the wings. Whether they reach a single person more than we're already doing, we'll have to see.

Thursday, 7 June 2018
Aaaaaaagain, it's my Edinburgh Fringe Programme Review

The annual treat of reading and digesting the Edinburgh Fringe programme is once more upon us, and yet again it thrills in a way that's impossible to describe to anyone who's never been. As readers of this blog will know, we first went to the Fringe in 1984*, and have been looking back at that programme and its successors virtually every year since. (*As punters, that is. I first took a show, The Sitcom Trials, up in 2001, and the Scottish Falsetto Socks made their Edinburgh debut in 2007).

The growth of the massive programme for this, the World's Biggest Art Festival - Official, has stalled. From 1984's 74 page programme to 2015's 440 pages, I noted that the guide had been growing an average of 20 pages a year. However last year (2017) it weighed in at 458 pages, which is exactly the same as this year. Shock horror, the Fringe isn't growing out of control!

What size the Comedy section? It's 142 pages, exactly the same as last year. (At which point I had to double check I wasn't reading last

considerably, in favour of musical comedy and variety. Competition will be stiffer this year between be-sequinned and heavily-made-up hoofers and harmonisers than at any time I can remember. It's apt that the highest profusion of camp shows are taking place in the Assembly Gardens' row of tents.

So to the parade of the best punny show titles. Here's my favourite 15:

year's prog. I'm not). Comedy reached a peak of 143 pages in 2012, dipping to 137 in 2015, but much of this variation is down to the amount of ad space taken. The first year I had a show on, 2001, there were 33 pages of comedy. In 1984 the subjects weren't separated out, but comedy seems to have accounted for only a few pages worth.

What has mushroomed in 2018 is Variety. 1984's programme listed such categories as Revue, Cabaret and even Mime, all giving Theatre and Comedy a run for their money. 34 years later, cabaret, burlesque, drag and various other performance genres have returned in force.

Assembly in particular seem to have dropped stand up

Brexit Through The Gift Shop - Matt Forde
Carey Carey Quite Contrary - Carey Marx
A Few Good Jen - Jenny Collier
Gagster's Paradise - Gary Delaney
Twat Out Of Hell - Gary G Knightley
Slattery Will Get You Nowhere - Tony Slattery
Thea-Skot Through The Heart & You're To Blame - Alison Thea-Skot
There's No i in Idiot - Olaf Falafel
Last Night A Weegie Saved My Life - Matt Price
Speaky Blinder - Chris McCausland
Bra Trek - Charmian Hughes
The Art Of The Dil - Dilruk Jayasinha
A Kealy's Heel - Alex Kealy

Float Like A Butterfly, John Hastings Like A Bee - John Hastings
See Novellie, Hear Novellie, Speak Novellie - Pierre Novellie

And my favourite?

All I Wanna Do is [FX: GUNSHOTS] With a [FX: GUN RELOADING] and [FX: CASH REGISTER] and Perform Some Comedy! - John-Luke Roberts

Sadly I couldn't include Josh Glanc's **Karma Karma Karma Karma Karma Chamedia**n because last year Mickey Sharma beat him to the punch with the slightly punnier Sharma Sharma Sharma Sharma Sharma Comedian. I'm sure both shows are great, so do please come and go. (Do you see what I did there?)

Black Lightning

A brand new song and video from the Scottish Falsetto Socks, destined to be part of the audience-in music for the new show SUPERHEROES. Black Lightning, sung to a familiar tune, as is our wont. As well as appearing on Youtube in this form, it is on Facebook in its square frame. Which, if any, gets watched is in the hands of fate.

Thursday, 7 June 2018
Hi Ho Silver Surfer

Another new video from the Socks, as to be featured in the audience-in music for the new show SUPERHEROES, which will be knocking them dead in Edinburgh throughout August. It's a song about The Silver Surfer, with a tune you might recognise. We've kept it brief, I hope you enjoy it. And, check it out, there's a new fangled square version too.

Monday, 11 June 2018

DC Song - A new song from the the Socks' Superheroes show - The DC Song. This will be forming part of the audience-in music and is one I'm particularly fond of.

DC they make good comics
They make Vertigo and other stuff too
Though their movies are usually poo
They're pretty good – DC

Way back in the day they made
Batman, Superman, Wonder Woman and
The Justice League, Green Lantern, and Green Arrow and the Flash and Aquaman
Their characters are varied and some are Octegnerian
That means they've been around for 80 years

DC - We love DC cos they made
Watchmen, they made Sandman, and John Constantine,
They made Swamp Thing, who's made out of slime, and published by DC

DC They'd so many characters, they did Crisis on Infinite Earths
Also the New 52 and DC Rebirth because they are DC
And the worst thing is that you've no idea what we're on about
Cos you've never read a single comic, specially not ones by DC

Friday, 8 June 2018

SOCKS COMIC - BE A SUPERHERO

The Scottish Falsetto Socks (and their pal Kev F out of The Beano) have produced a very special item to accompany the new show Superheroes: The Official SUPERHEROES COMIC!

It's 24 pages long and features brand new comic adaptations of Socks Superheroes songs & sketches, some that are in the show and some that aren't, including Superman, The Avengers, Batman, Black Panther, Deadpool and lots more.

And we would like you to be part of it.

You can become a Socks

Superhero, have your name in the comic, and have a unique Sock drawing by Kev F, all as part of helping us get it out there. Here's what we'd like to offer you:

BE A SOCK HERO - £15

For £15 you'll get a signed copy of the comic, and your name will be featured in the list of Sock Heroes, being read out loud (ok, in a voice bubble) by The Scottish Falsetto Socks, on the inside front page of the Socks Superhero Comic.

BE A SOCK SUPERHERO - £30

For £30 you get two signed copies of the comic, and your name will be featured with its own Individual Sock Drawing by Kev F on the inside front page of the Socks Superhero Comic.
 - You get to choose which superhero you'd like a Sock dressed as!
 - And you get the original line drawing too!

(Eg Here you can see Fanny De Sauchs has chosen a Sock to be drawn as Wolverine. Yes it does.)

Sock Heroes and Sock Superheroes can order additional copies of the comic at £3 each when you make your contribution. The comics will only be available to the general public at Socks Superheroes previews & at the Edinburgh Fringe in August, at £3 a copy.

This is a Very Short Notice Offer, ending at midnight on Tuesday June 12th (because we need to get the artwork completed and sent to the printers) so please act fast if

you want to be included.

To become a Sock Hero or Superhero, simply send your contribution by PayPal to sockpuppets@sitcomtrials.co.uk and include the vital details - your name (as it should appear in the comic), and which Superhero you'd like drawn (if you're going for the Superhero option).

Deadline midnight Tuesday June 12th 2018.

NB: The only other special item we're producing for this year's show is the Socks Superhero t-shirt, which Kickstarter pledgers will get notice of first. You'll be able to buy it before it goes on sale in Edinburgh.

Thanks & lots of love from The Socks

Kev F Sutherland
Scottish Falsetto Sock Puppet Theatre
kevf.sutherland@gmail.com
Tweet @falsettosocks
Facebook ScottishFalsettoSocks

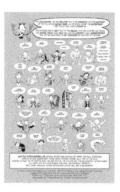

Saturday, 16 June 2018
Thanks everyone - Sock comic in production

With the greatest of all possible thanks to the wonderful Socks fans who pitched in over the weekend, the Scottish Falsetto Socks' Superheroes comic has gone to the printers. Above you can see the drawings I've done for every one of the sponsors. They'll be getting the original drawing along with signed copies of the comic itself when it emerges next week.

Everyone else will have to wait till they come to a Socks show to be able to get their hands on a copy, though they will be available to the public in the fullness of time. In the meantime, here are some tasty titbits to enjoy.

Sunday, 17 June 2018
St Buttcheek Stinklesburg - comics by kids

My favourite title of the season has come from kids at a half term workshop at G Live in Guildford. Saint Buttcheek Stinklesburg was such a novel name that I was sure it must come from a game or a meme, but it would seem to have sprung fully formed from the imagination of an 11 year old, which should give us great hope for the youth of our nation.

At Red Oaks primary in Swindon, the year 6s were doing a topic on Stonehenge which they took great delight in rubbishing for their comic's title. Meanwhile the next class came up with a fine title, for which I produced one of my most disappointing covers. I can hardly use the excuse that I draw these quickly, whole the class is going on. Sometimes I churn out a corker, and sometimes I produce a real "I wish there was time to rub it out and start again", which is what you see on the right.

My annual visit to Ruskin primary in Swindon, which I have been doing for quite possibly ten years now, produced another couple of corking titles, though I can't say I'm

impressed by my attempt to draw Declan Donelly. The live caricatures I do of the kids have about an 80% likeness rate, I'd say. I draw up to 60 every day, so that's not bad going. But give me five minutes with a photo of a celebrity and somehow their obvious features elude me. I googled and drew an accurate Ghostbusters firehouse though, so I wasn't slouching.

My second day at Ruskin saw the first instance I can remember of me getting the giggles. I mean really bad giggles. I got the giggles so bad, while reading out the kids' suggestions for the title of the

comic, that my eyes were streaming with tears. All because one of the suggestions someone had written was "I'm Your Fammy", which I read out, accidentally in a hurry, as "I'm Your Fanny". Being year 6, only a couple spotted this or reacted with amused shock, but it was stifling the desire to refer to it, or to explain it away, that triggered the giggles. I was still chuckling at the memory of it on the way home.

The celebrities these 7 groups chose to appear in my demonstration strip were Donald Trump (twice), Kim Kardashian, Simon Cowell, Kim Jong Un, Gordon Ramsay, and Bruce Willis.

Tuesday, 19 June 2018
Chortle & Young Perspective
interviews

In the promotional run up to
Edinburgh, the Socks have
completed a couple of email
interviews. They gave their
answers to Young Perspective
magazine in the form of a video
(which they may or may not use)...

And here are my Chortle answers.
Let's see which, if any, ever make
the website.

The Big Ask 2018 The
questions... Don't feel you have to
answer them all. Each day we'll
feature one question and the best
answers

**Describe the Edinburgh Fringe in
5 words** One damn thing after

another

**Who have the Edinburgh
comedy award judges most
heinously overlooked over the
years?** Er *cough* hello?

**What's your favourite joke from
your show?** My friend had to
accept a TV award even though
she was really ill. Emmy? No, she
just had a bad cold.

**Which comedian past or present
would perfectly complement you
as a double-act partner** Max
Wall. Cos then all our responses
would be off the... you can finish
that gag off yourself

**What's the best performance
space at the Fringe and why?**
You can't beat the open air,
especially for Shakespeare. We

saw Dannii Minogue doing open air Shakespeare one year, when it was quite windy. The best thing? Couldn't hear a word.

What track do you walk on to and why? Respect by Aretha Franklin. We've looped the bit that goes "Sock it to me". For obvious reasons.

What's the weirdest Fringe show you've ever seen and why? Once saw a performance act doing their show in a doorway on the Royal Mile. Had his back turned to the audience then did what can only be described as a wee. Wasn't a big audience, just myself. Quite an influential act though, I've seen tribute versions every year since.

What do you plan to do on your day off? Only wimps have a day off. We've not had a day off at Edinburgh in the ten years we've been doing this. We're knackered.

What's the worst place you've ever stayed at the Fringe? One year I stayed in a room at a musician's place where the corridors were lined with a mix of dust bunnies and cat shit, for which he didn't charge any extra, so there was that.

What are your plans once the Fringe is over? Genuinely we've been booked at do a week of shows in Denmark, on the condition that we do 20 minutes about Brexit. So we'll be writing a new show.

What's the worst room to perform in at the Fringe and why? There's a doorway on the Royal Mile which is really rubbish if you're on after the bloke who does the wee (I think he's called Lost Bladder Control Guy).

Can you come up with an advertising slogan to get people to the Fringe? Come to Embra, the month before Septembra

What gets you through Edinburgh's toughest days? The ability to power snooze. Sometimes back in the flat, sometimes during my fellow performers' shows. For which I apologise in advance.

What's the oddest prop you've bought or had made for a Fringe show? Looks in this year's prop bag, sees clockwork teeth, rubber Batman, bag of dog poo. Has difficulty conceiving of what's odd any more

Who is the best person you've ever met at Edinburgh?

Benedict Cumberbatch. He stole the Socks. At the bar of the Gilded Balloon he inadvertently started walking off with the bag that had the moist and smelly post-show Sock puppets in, thinking it was his friends. Had a very enjoyable half hour chat with pre-fame "call me Ben".

What's your enduring memory from the first Fringe you ever went to?

It was mind blowingly big, the biggest event I'd ever seen. And given that this was in the 1980s, when the comedy section took up about two pages of the programme, this suggests I had a smaller mind than the kids today.

What's the most you've put into the bucket of a free show and why were you so generous?

Five quid. Too embarrassed to ask for change.

What is the one thing you know now that you wish you'd known before your first Fringe?

The value of a good photograph. Back in the pre selfie days we spent so much time enjoying the moment instead of recording it. Old folk, eh?

What do you think of critics?

Love them, especially that nice Mr Bennett from Chortle. (How many people have given that answer? Dozens? Or just the honest few)

If you could change one thing about the Fringe, what would it be?

Once I'd have said I wish the press would cover a wider range of venues to review their comedy at. Now I'm just grateful there's any press left at all. (But if the Comedy Award and the Guardian spend all their time at The Pleasance again, I will continue to moan about it).

What's the most drunk or otherwise wasted you've ever been at the Fringe?

At these prices? And with the minimum alcohol price in force this year you can expect a record number of boringly sober comedians. The bars are very grateful for all the posh Londoners in rugby shirts who think the bar prices are "pretty reasonable compared to the rest of

Scandinavia".

Who is the worst person you've ever met at Edinburgh?

Did I mention Lost Bladder Control Guy? I asked what his show was called. Apparently it was called Fuck Off You Pervy Bastard. That'll be why it wasn't in the programme.

What's the oddest thing you've read in a Fringe review of yourself or others?

One or two reviews have forgotten to put the right number of stars on, the idiots.

Who or what inspired you to get into comedy?

Like so many people, it was bullying at school. I found a torrent of abysmal puns was a brilliant bullying technique.

Has the 'spirit of the Fringe' been lost?

No, that's the Spirit Of St Louis you're thinking of. And it wasn't lost, it was Lindbergh's baby that was lost. And Amelia Earhart. And Flight 19. But not the Spirit Of The Fringe, I'm happy to say.

Who is the unsung hero of the Fringe and why?

It's a toss up between Yehudi

Menuhin and David Frost. Menuhin attempted to stage the first Free Fringe shows in the 1950s as a spin off from the Official Festival, and David Frost staged the first late night cabarets with TV names in the 1960s, and attracted the TV. (I've read a bit too much about the history of the Fringe, sorry.)

What's the oddest thing you've found in your bucket at the end of a free show?

Never done a free show.

What's the worst Fringe review you ever had?

A one star review of my old show The Sitcom Trials. "I'd have happily gouged my own eyes with hot spoons rather than endure another moment." We put that up outside the box office, it doubled the audience from then on. Who wouldn't want to see that show?

Tuesday, 19 June 2018
Socks make gifs

God help us, I've found another way of trying in vain to grab peoples attention on Twitter - gifs. Using an app called Giphly, I'm able to grab bits of videos and make little gifs of them, for the world to ignore. Here are my first efforts.

Tuesday, 19 June 2018
Happy is a man who's got his graph back

I recently had my laptop re-zhoozhed (how DO you spell that word? To zhoozh something up? Anyway, that's how I spell it) by Tantra computers, so I now have the latest operating system, which means all my programmes have had to be re-installed. And some are reinstalled more successfully than others. I've already had fun trying to open old Quark Xpress docs in the new version for example (I have to use the 2016 version to open the Socks performance scripts now), and the latest glitch I've found is with Microsoft Word.

I've essentially been using and updating the same Graph of my Socks sales figures for Edinburgh since I made it back in 2007. It's travelled through two, maybe three laptops, and who knows how many upgrades. But this time it was just failing to open. For a couple of weeks I've been trying and getting frustrated, and meanwhile I've been able to see my sales figures for Edinburgh - via the wonderful Red61 system - trickling in since sometime back in April (it may even

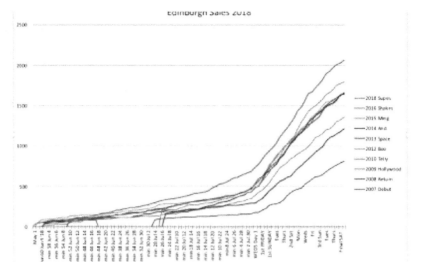

have been March. Tickets have definitely been on sale for longer this year than ever before). In short I was desperate to get those figures turned into a graph.

And so it was that, this week, I went back to square one and started a brand new Chart in Microsoft Excel. The only way I could access my past ten years of sales figures was to open the old graph on my old laptop - the white MacBook that I replaced in 2014 - take screen grabs of the figures and print them out. I then had to type in manually every daily sales figure for every Socks show since 2007 till the present day. And do you know what, it was quite therapeutic. And fun to know that I have a chart that, for this year at least, works.

And the best news? 2018's Superheroes show is currently outselling 2016's Shakespeare show at the same point that year. As you'll remember from graph analyses gone by, ever since 2013 our shows have ended up selling pretty much exactly the same number of tickets by the end of August. But there's always the potential for more, so let's make this year the great big biggie shall we?

Thursday, 21 June 2018
Superhero Preview Ludlow June 20

It's been nearly a month between previews, but we've spent the time well. Admittedly most of that was spent making the Superheroes comic, but some time's been spent rejigging the show, and last night's test showed that we're getting there. A very small audience (on a Wednesday, in Ludlow, up against James Acaster starting at exactly the same time) but they were very good, giving just the test we needed and laughing where we wanted them to. Lots of things have moved since last time, a song's been shortened, and we've lost & replaced the Spiderman/Peter Parker song. This is what we gave them.

SUPERHEROES RUNNING ORDER, Weds June 20 2018

(All items good as before unless mentioned)

Opening Batman/Ditko/Flash - slight tweak now even better
I'm A Sock song
Cosmopolitan / Bob Kane
Motion Capture
Scottish Superheroes - moved from later in show, good move
Hulk Ang Lee
Plot/ Maguffin
Batman/ Teeth / etc - moved from later in show, good move

NEW Bechdel Test song - brilliant. So glad I came up with this
Cock Robin
Science/Faraday/Sagan

NEW Helium routine - very good, that's staying
Brother 1
Racist Brother song
Avengers
Avengers Reel
Dr Strange / Wong / Thanos

NEW Wonder Woman routine - good
NEW Fantastic 4 - recast & rewritten, works much better
Thanos / Who's On First
Superman / JorEl / Kents / Glasses
Dead Ringer song

Brother 2
Science 2
Joker 2
Harley & Ivy
Daredevil - decided this will be cut from the show, not good enough
Brother 3 - needs shortening
What I've Learned - needs shortening

NEW All By Myself song - now shortened, much much better
NEW Finale - now short and fast and worked. By golly, our show has an ending!

And we have a new Preview date lined up, on July 5th in Harrow, meaning we have five shows left to polish the hour. At time of writing (the morning after the show) I've already put a new-ish song back into the show, one that we haven't done in these previews but that appears in the comic and that I did back in 2016 and belatedly realise could be perfect. Stay tuned for how that goes down in a couple of weeks time.

Thursday, 21 June 2018
Daredevil

Another one bites the dust, in this case Daredevil, which is another bit of material that's been cut from the Socks' new show Superheroes. It seemed a funny idea at the time, but it never really took shape, and the only laughs came from the costume, for reasons you can probably see. Please enjoy the costume's moment in the sun. It will be being dismantled and its components recycled by the time you've finished watching the clip.

Thursday, 28 June 2018
Thor & Odin
This is a gag that I first did in one of my comic strips, in something like UT, Gag, Blag, Gas or some such comic of the time, at least 25 years ago, so I'm making no claims for novelty here. But I've always liked the gag and, though it's not made it into the show, it works well as a short video. If only more people watched these things than come and see us live, eh?

Friday, 22 June 2018
Getting paranoid about portraits

A small thing maybe, but I've been sent into the weekend in quite a paranoid state of mind having received a Friday afternoon email from a school I visited recently. It's a school I've visited a number of times over the years, doing my Comic Art Masterclasses, as part of which every child has their caricature drawn. The caricatures, which take a minute each, are probably the most popular and sought-after part of the class, with many teachers also clamouring to be drawn, and my work being exhibited and displayed on walls and school reports in my wake.

So my heart sank when I read, from a school which I won't name, the following.

We wanted to share and highlight some recent feedback from a parent in relation to the Caricatures drawn. As you are aware they tend to highlight and draw out certain features of a person and we have been made aware this has created insecurities this time around for some of the children recently drawn.

We are very much looking forward to your return next year at (the school) but feel it would be best if we do not do the Caricatures in class next time to avoid this happening again, I hope you understand our reasons for requesting this.

Not do the caricatures? Because of something said, by the sound of it, by one parent of one pupil who, by next year, won't even be at the school? They're seriously asking that, after nearly ten years of making an annual two day visit to the same school, over which time I've drawn about 900 childrens' caricatures, they should deny next year's Year 6s (the current Year 5s) the chance to take away this treasured item, that their brothers and sisters already have, all because of a parent of a kid who isn't even there any more?

You won't be surprised that my blood's boiling at the moment. And my mood hasn't been helped been the words of consolation from the Head who, when I protested, let me know that:

I was simply responding to a concerned parent who shared a social media thread with me. On it there were a number of posts from parents, past and present, who had commented on your visit. Although they thought what you did was fantastic, a number of them claimed that their children were made to feel self-conscious of features that had been exaggerated for the purpose of the caricatures.

"Social media thread"???? There are parents, more than one, talking about me and my caricatures behind my back? Where? What are they saying? This is horrifying.

I am looking forward to a paranoid weekend, scouring Twitter and Facebook trying to find who's bad-mouthing me, and the dreadful things they're saying about me. I am really worried that people could be saying untruths about my caricatures and that this could affect me work at other schools.

For over a decade I've been spending about 100 days a year teaching about 60 kids a day, and drawing all their faces. That's 60,000 faces drawn without a

single complaint. Now some parents from one school have got me paranoid that there's something wrong with my work, and a school is threatening to not let me do that part of my class. I guess I just won't be returning to that school again. But, god, I seriously hope this isn't something that's going to spread.

Look at the pictures above. Those are the kids I drew at that school when I visited. Who could have a complaint about those pictures?

Yours, a paranoid artist.

Chortle Perfect Playlist by The Socks

Here comedians choose half-a-dozen or so of their favourite comedy moments, illustrated with clips. Whether it's just the things that make them laugh or important influences on their careers, these selections reveal what makes their comedy brains tick.

Thursday, 28 June 2018
Bechdel Test - new from the Socks

Brand new from the Socks, two superheroes try and pass The Bechdel Test. Enjoy.

This sketch hasn't made it into the show, though the song that goes with it has. Stay tuned for that if you see the show live, or when it makes its way online after the show's had its time in Edinburgh. This is a lovely bit of fun and I do hope people like it.

The Scottish Falsetto Sock Puppet Theatre pick their perfect playlist from their favourite comedy double acts. It's our tenth year doing a brand new show at the Edinburgh Fringe, so it's about time we fessed up and revealed the comedy acts off whom we ripped our act. Though every line we write is sparklingly original and fresh from our hard-working comedy brains, it's hard to help noticing all these other acts who, spookily, did most of our schtick first.

Bob & Terry, The Likely Lads
You know that routine the Socks do in every show where one of us mishears a word the other one's said and it spirals through a series of similar misunderstandings to a hilarious conclusion? Yes you do. Oh come on, we've done it in every

bloody show. Well, it turns out (we find, having seen it repeated on Yesterday) we totally lifted that from Whatever Happened To The Likely Lads. Also the whole Aspirational One v Complacent One schtick. Thanks Clements & LaFrenais.

Peter Cook & Dudley Moore
There's no shame in admitting you're wallowing in the shadow of two of the most respected comedians in history. Although what we took from Pete & Dud wasn't the sparkling wit or the accomplished piano playing. It was what Cook called Happy Amateurism, which was his excuse for being an alcoholic and our excuse for perennial underachievement. And corpsing. We took that from them too.

Peter Glaze & Don Maclean

History has largely forgotten this pair, who live on only in the memory of people of a certain age. They were the comedy stars of Crackerjack, on children's BBC from the mid 70s to the early 80s, by which time Glaze, who had been a member of The Crazy Gang in the 50s, was already one of the oldest people I'd ever seen on the telly. He's the guy who coined "D'oh", which sadly Homer Simpson went on to own. As a double act they perfected the Cheeky One constantly getting the rise out of the Uptight One, and Crackerjack ended every week with a musical parody. Sometimes they changed the lyrics, but the songs were at their most satisfactory when they just sang them straight. I say straight...

The Two Ronnies Gerald Wiley, aka Ronnie Barker, may be the

single most influential writer on our work. He did word play which may have become unfashionable in subsequent years but stands the test of time, and did the best Putting Words To Other Peoples Songs there is.

National Theatre Of Brent Why doesn't everyone know the National Theatre Of Brent? Now riding high on the success of The 39 Steps, Patrick Barlow's Desmond Olivier Dingle was the ultimate Uptight Guy Who's Trying To Put On A Play. And Jim Broadbent, now way famouser than Patrick Barlow in a way that nobody would have predicted back the the National Theatre Of Brent's heyday, was the best Dopey Sidekick ever. "Might ine ask" is a phrase still used regularly in our home. If you've never seen the NTOB, that will mean nothing to you. On the plus side, though, you'll think the Scottish Falsetto

Sock Puppet Theatre totally invented our way of doing Shakespeare parodies and historic re-enactions.

Mr Show with Bob & Dave Mr Show wasn't, strictly, an influence on The Socks because, to be honest, we'd been going for five years before we even knew it existed. But it pre-dates us, so it counts. And has some of the most out-of-the-box original double-act sketch work we've ever seen.

Abbott & Costello If there had never been a Scottish Falsetto Sock Puppet Theatre then history would have to settle for these guys. I mean, contrived word play? Histrionic over acting in a high pitched voice? A straight guy who never gets a laugh? It's okay. We're here now, you never have to watch these guys ever ag - Third Base!

Friday, 29 June 2018
Superheroes Flyer & Poster
designed at last

At long last, and much later then in
previous years, I've got the new
flyers and posters artworked for our
Edinburgh show. 2015's were
completed in the April of that year
(according to this blog, which
shows all the previous flyers going
back to 2007), but this year I've
somehow not got round to it till
now. (2016's flyer doesn't get
blogged till August, so maybe I've
not been so tardy this year after
all). I'm particularly pleased with
the back of the flyer.

The artwork, which I coloured
specially, is from the splash page
of the Socks Superheroes comic,
which will be on sale at the Fringe,
I hope (I'm sitting on nearly 500
copies, so we'd better start shifting
them soon). Whether its
resemblance to the Infinity War
poster has retained any currency I
don't know, but I think it represents
the show well and should be fun to
hand out at the rate of 300 a day.

I'd been struggling with the poster,
trying to make it look more exciting
and superheroic without cluttering
it. I have a variety of other socks

cartoon figures to use, but it
became too busy when I stuck
them in. So I went with lightning,
which seems to have done the
trick.

I've put in a bid for a big A1 poster
outside the venue, though they're
reserving those spaces for the
shows in bigger rooms than me.
Still, it would be great if I could
have one and artwork a character-
filled border to go with it. Let's see.

Saturday, 30 June 2018
Celery & Constipation - comics and flipcharts by kids

June has been the quietest month of the year for my Comic Art Masterclasses, being the height of exam season and with no Bank Holidays or half terms to fill. But inbetween working hard at my desk producing the Socks comic and finalising the show, I've managed a few days at the chalkface. These two examples are from Dean Close School in Cheltenham.

It was a long hot six and a half hour drive to Felixstowe for these two classes, but well worth it they were. Thanks to the Felixstowe Book Festival for laying on these sessions at the library.

This month saw a couple of events

where I was invited to give a talk, but not to do the full class. So on both these occasions - at Croome House in Worcestershire, and a park in Maidenhead - I had lots of spare time on my hands in which to turn out a nice page of flipchart for them to keep. The examples above are from Croome, which was Beano themed as you can tell, and Dean Close school where my classes had a late start cos the kids had to get their innoculations. The one below was Maidenhead's flipchart.

At Ludlow Fringe I did one class on the afternoon ahead of doing the Socks show in the evening, and here's what they produced.

The celebrities these 5 groups chose to appear in my demonstration strip were Kim Jong Un, David Attenborough, Donald Trump (twice), and Tom Holland. PLUS - an added bonus - I did three talks (in Maidenhead and Croome) which didn't involve making a comic but did involve the demo strip, for which those three groups chose Simon Cowell, David Walliams, and Mary Berry.

Tuesday, 3 July 2018
New Socks Superheroes t shirt - available now

Here it is at last, the 2018 Scottish Falsetto Sock Puppet Theatre: SUPERHEROES Official t-shirt and it can be yours now! Ready to post now! Am I using too many exclamation marks?!?

It's our traditional black t shirt, available in Small, Medium, Large, XL, XXL, and Female Medium, bearing the new Socks Superheroes roundel (detail below,

clearly fake shirt in photo above)

To order one, simply pay £20 (UK) /$30 (to USA) by Paypal to sockpuppets@sitcomtrials.co.uk including in your order the size you want and your full address. A shirt will be yours by return.

The print run has been made, so sizes are limited to the ones shown above (thanks to those who pre-ordered kids sizes and super-duper-large shirts, those are now sadly out of stock). In Edinburgh the shirts will be £15 each direct from me (ie postage free).

Thanks in anticipation for your orders. Love The Socks.

NB: Postage. Two shirts are £35 / $50 inc postage, three shirts are £52 / $75 inc postage, four shirts are £70 / $100 inc postage.

Here's the actual shirt itself (though this time it's the Socks that are fake):

Friday, 6 July 2018
Quad posters and Harrow preview

I think it's been 10 years since I paid to have posters displayed on the streets of Edinburgh during the Fringe. Way back in 2007 there was a company called Diabolical Liberties who did it. We celebrated them in song in fact. (With a video that's not aged well...)

Back then it was the last days of flyposting when, as we say in the song, "a man with a bucket and a big fat brush" would stick your posters on any available surface. This was, obviously, rather destructive to the look of Edinburgh, and you'd find remnants of many of these posters clinging to their various surfaces when you returned a year later.

So it was that the council and the venues and promoters got together and got the distribution of posters officially licensed, and every year since it's got a bit more professional, and a bit more expensive. Ten years ago I paid £250 to get (I think) 100 A2 posters flyposted all over Edinburgh. This year I decided to dip my toe in the water and found, for £150, I could afford to have two posters put up.

They are, it has to be said, quite big (Quad size, which is 30" x 40") and printed on thick vinyl, and attached properly to specially erected stands. But, blimey, the amount some companies are paying for posters is mind boggling. I'm perfectly aware that my tiny drop in the ocean will go unseen among the millions, but if they put 15 and a half bums on seats, then they've justified their investment. (That's fifteen bums and one buttock, and don't think I won't be counting).

Oh yeah, and we did another Preview of Superheroes, and it went brilliantly. Too soon to be getting cocky, but I think, short of a few nips and tucks, we have the show that we'll be keeping. We were on at the Trinity Bar in Harrow, and many thanks to Alison Kent for putting this on. We didn't get a big audience - this being the hottest summer for years, and most people being more interested in football than going to comedy shows - but the dozen or so in the room gave us a marvellous reception, and a perfect test of our stuff. There were only two people who'd seen us before, and so we won over a handful of strangers then really made them laugh with all Superheroes and no fallback stuff.

The running order is now:

SUPERHEROES RUNNING ORDER, Thurs July 5 2018
(All items good as before unless mentioned)

Opening Batman/Ditko/Flash I'm A Sock song

Cosmopolitan / Bob Kane
NEW - Wonderful World song -
Perfect! Why hasn't this been in the
show all along?
Motion Capture
Scottish Superheroes
Hulk Ang Lee
Plot/ Maguffin
Batman/ Teeth / etc
Bechdel Test song
NEW - Joker calls Harley & Ivy -
good, works
Cock Robin
Science/Faraday/Sagan
Helium routine

Brother 1
Racist Brother song
Avengers
Avengers Reel
Dr Strange / Wong / Thanos
Wonder Woman routine
Fantastic 4
Superman / JorEl / Kents /
Glasses
Dead Ringer song
Brother 2
Science 2
Joker 2
Harley & Ivy
Brother 3 - now shorter
What I've Learned - now shorter
All By Myself song
NEW Finale - with extra Thanos,
even better.

The show came to about an hour &
ten minutes last night, with a lot of
audience play (we adlibbed Saltire
Man from audience suggestion and
had some good banter) so we can
lose a lot still. If anything it's the
Brother subplot that's now not as
funny as the superhero material,
which is pretty much the opposite
of where we were back in March.
I'll just keep trimming as we go,
and hopefully the adlibs and banter
will bed in while the structure stays
the same. Well done us. (Cue the
next preview being horrible and me
wanting to rewrite the whole thing.
Wouldn't be the first time.)

Tuesday, 10 July 2018
Chuffing Wazzocks - new comics by kids

If it's the latest hottest weekend of the year, then it must see me spending three days in Scunthorpe. Thanks to the smashing 2021 Art Centre, I had an extended trip, which included staying in a hotel with a view of the Humber Bridge and lakes all round. V pleasant. One thing I was up against, for my class at Scunthorpe Library on Saturday afternoon, was the England v Sweden World Cup Quarter Final. Amazingly we attracted a class of 12 and did a fine class. On kid, oddly, was wearing a football shirt but wasn't bothered about the football. I shall be hoping this same syndrome extends to Welsh comedy fans when, this coming Wednesday, The Scottish Falsetto Socks attempt to do an Edinburgh Preview at the same time as the Semi Final.

The trip began with two Scunthorpe schools in a day. Well, to be accurate, it began with a 90 minute drive from a hotel on the M1 near Nottingham which came, in turn, after a drive from the Socks gig in Harrow which took three and a half hours (longer than it should). So these classes were managed on five hours sleep after five hours driving. Ironically they only added up to four hours of teaching.

Scunthrope's 2021 Visual Arts centre had organised the three day trip, and they got the final day's classes, on a hot and humid Sunday. Two more perfect classes, though I say so myself.

The timing of the two classes on the Friday meant that I had more time than usual on my hands to draw the flipchart. Sometimes I arrive in school just when we're about to start and getting nothing drawn. In this case, I arrived at a primary school at 8.30 in the morning and they didn't need me till 9.30, then in the afternoon at the secondary school I was there at midday and not needed till 1.30. So, a couple of nice looking flipcharts to leave them with.

At Scunthorpe Libray on the Saturday I gave them a tribute to Steve Ditko, whose death was only announced that morning. And on Sunday I took the opportunity to reference 2000AD comics - which hardly ever happens as no kid has ever heard of 2000AD and I haven't read it myself for ten years, sadly. It was too good an opportunity to miss to make the 2021 logo look like 2000AD's classic masthead.

It wasn't all Scunthorpe this week. There was also a one-off class at Coleford Library in The Forest Of Dean. Jolly good fun, and nice to work somewhere that doesn't take half a day to get to.

The celebs these seven groups chose to star in my demonstration strip were Kim Kardashian, Dwayne Johnson, Simon Cowell, David Walliams, Will Ferrell, Kim Jong Un, and, most original of the week, Sir Isaac Newton.

Friday, 13 July 2018
Bible The Sequel - comics by kids

This week's classes were blissfully short of long distance travel, indeed a couple of them could be classed a positively local. These two comics, produced at Bridlewood Primary school in Swindon and Swindon Academy, were a mere hour's drive away. Luxury. The Trump theme was a coincidence, but also notable that we've hardly ended up with a Trump cover for months, after the dozens we've had in the past year or two.

St Katherine's Academy in Pill, just 20 minutes from home, came up with a possibly contentious title with Bible The Sequel, and also another of the many Pineapple titles that occasionally crop up. Pineapples and potatoes are the most popular edible subject matter for kids comic, for reasons I can't fathom.

What did I say? This post-school session at Neath Comedy Festival gave us another potato classic. And the next day at Churchill Academy (again, just 20 minutes drive from home), which was an all day class with one group, was the first of the summer to mention the World Cup. The day after England got knocked out, and they come up with a cover rubbing it in. Kids eh?

I produced a couple of good flipcharts this week, maybe not as busy as the ones I managed the previous week. But this one from Churchill managed to include Gareth Southgate and his characteristic waistcoat from the World Cup. The other one's from St Katherines in Pill.

The celebrities these 6 groups chose to appear in my demonstration strip were John Travolta, David Beckham, Boris Johnson, Taylor Swift, Kim Jong Un, and Theresa May.

Tuesday, 17 July 2018
Animated gifs and Neath Preview

The Socks Superhero Preview in Neath on July 11th was the most surprising for the very fact that it took place.

Having done a Comic Art Masterclass in the afternoon, I was quite prepared for the evening show to be cancelled taking place, as it did, slap bang in the middle of England v Croatia in the World Cup Semi Final, England's most important football match for 28 years. As it happened I needn't have worried. Neath is a rugby town, in the valleys in Wales, and no-one gives a toss about either the English or football, so I got a bigger audience than last week in Harrow. About twice the size in fact.

(Here, have an animated gif. This was my first attempt at trying to look like a 3D lenticular. I'm sure I'll master it in time.)

The Neath crowd was mostly folks who'd seen the Socks before so were very supportive, but also a good test of when material wasn't as strong as the rest. As a result of which I was going through the whole show thinking "this bit goes on too long", and "this is good, we need to build on that", etc.

So we were doing exactly the same script as Harrow, and I'm now sat at my desk script-editing. Having run through the script, and all the prop changes, with the fully erected fully propped socks' set in my office, my various notes go:

Motion Capture - needs tightening
Ang Lee - needs shortening
Batman - needs to build on audience interaction
Various costume changes - need off-stage banter to cover
Joker calling Harley and Ivy - now has a new prop, and is separated into two scenes
Doctor Strange - needs more action
The Kents - need tightening
Falling out scene - needs callbacks
Final Brother scene - shorten
Finale - more callbacks

So, Bedford Fringe on Thursday should get the best script ever. I hope they're ready for it.

Saturday, 21 July 2018
Man Made Of Bottoms, and Simon Cowell - comics by kids

What's more delightful, on the cover of a comic book created with a group of schoolkids, than a unicorn climbing up a rainbow lamppost? Well the answer, obviously, is seahorses, fire extinguishers and a man made of bottoms. What are the chances that two of the most delightful things should come from classes in Hemel Hempstead library?

From the air conditioned luxury of Hemel, on the hottest day of the year (NB this being the 30th consecutive hottest days-of-the-year of the year), it was up the road to the Latitude Festival where the kids and I produced these two comics in a tent. Then didn't actually produce them as there was no photocopier. Cos we were in a tent, in a field, on the hottest day of the year (31st consecutive thereof).

In Enniskillen, in contrast, it was quite cloudy and overcast. But the kids were as brilliant as ever, and their comics equally so. Though, I'm told, Kill It With Fire is a "dead meme". Me neither.

The celebrities these 6 groups chose to appear in my demonstration strip were Simon Cowell (a career-resurgently three times), Jake Paul, Tom Cruise, and - best suggestion of the month - William The Conqueror.

Tuesday, 24 July 2018
Happy happy sales sales, and travels with my art

I'm fully aware of the fact I'm overly obsessed with my sales figures at this time of year, in the run up to Edinburgh, but you can allow me a few indulgent smiles of joy as I look at my graph at the moment. Though these things can turn on a sixpence, right now Superheroes is

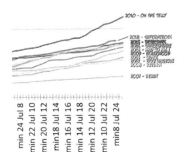

min 24 Jul 8 min 22 Jul 10 min 20 Jul 12 min18 Jul 14 min 16 Jul 16 min 14 Jul 18 min 12 Jul 20 min 10 Jul 22 min8 Jul 24

our second best selling show - at this stage in the run-up - ever.

Last week it overtook 2015's Minging Detectives, which I see from blogs of the time was riding high having had some high profile previews, including nice photo pieces in the Welsh papers and in Metro, and ahead of last year's Shakespeare. Of course all this decade's shows have ended up tying for total sales in the end, let's just hope Superheroes keeps up with that.

(As previously noted, we've never since compared with 2010's record sales, when we had a show on in a 9.15 slot - the primiest of primetime - and had notched up record TV appearances and reviews, with a Youtube videoing trending into the bargain. As always, hope springs

eternal).

Of course it maybe these animated gifs that are helping. You would tell me if was overdoing it with these things, wouldn't you?

The big news at the moment is that Mum's not very well, so Jude has been visiting her a lot and I've been visiting as much as I can. Her chemo earlier in the year was making her feel bad, so they changed the dose which made her feel worse, and in the last couple of weeks she's found it's spread so she's needing fresh radiotherapy. She's had a couple of falls and is needing a lot more help and attention, pretty well round the clock. We're hoping she's going to see some improvement, but obviously I've picked a rather unhelpful time to be shooting off to Edinburgh for a month.

My travels, during this, the hottest driest summer since 1969 (yes, who knew 69 was drier than the famous 76 of our childhoods?) took me to Enniskillen over the weekend (where it's not all that hot or dry, compared to the South Of England), and as I write this I'm in a busy week of Comic Art Masterclasses which goes

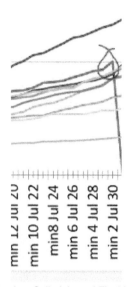

min 12 Jul 20 min 10 Jul 22 min8 Jul 24 min 6 Jul 26 min 4 Jul 28 min 2 Jul 30

for one day, before the start of our run. That's 35 tickets sold in a day. Once the show opens on Wednesday, you aim to do that and more every day. But in the run-up it's pretty impressive. Ooh, I loves my graph.

UPDATE: Weds Aug 1 10.45am. Hubris is your worst enemy. Never hubriscate. Hubriscation nej tak. Having boasted about my 35 sales on Monday, Tuesday almost flatlined with a feeble 13 sales. And as of Wednesday morning we've not sold a single ticket in twelve hours. Huuuuuubriiiis!

Monday: Colindale and Finchley Central, Tuesday: Worcester, Wednesday: Darlington and Crockerton, Thursday: Hartlepool and Stockton, Friday: Leyburn in North Yorkshire, Saturday: Woolaton and Sherwood in Nottingham, Saturday night: visiting Mum in Kibbie, Sunday: Socks previews in Derby and Sheffield, then Monday to Edinburgh. Enough miles for you?

UPDATE: Monday July 30th, the day Hev and I drove to Edinburgh, check this out:

It might not look much to you, but that's a record uptick in our sales

Friday, 27 July 2018
Aliens, Beer & Toothpaste - comics by kids

A busy stretch of comic art masterclasses in the run up to Edinburgh began in Barnet Libraries. Barnet is bigger than you realise, taking in 15 different libraries, so I hope I impressed them enough to have me back to the other 13. As it was, these two classics were the produce of

groups in Colindale and Finchley Central.

At The Hive in Worcester - and I'm seeing my fair share of shiny new library buildings this week I must say (Barnet's libraries included one you can't get into without a card and two sets of state-of-the-art electric security gates, while The Hive had hi-tech codes on all the doors right alongside a toilet door handle that had fallen off so no-one could lock it) - I worked with Greenfingers, who are cared-for kids of various backgrounds, all of whom were smashing.

Up the A1 to Darlington Library where we produced one comic in the morning with a sellout group, then to Cockerton Library in the afternoon for the same again. Great groups, and some well-promoted classes by Suzy at the library who's had me back a few times. It's good when your reputation grows and word gets about. Did I mention all of these classes have been tied into the Summer Reading Challenge's Mischief Makers project, which is Beano-themed this year? I could have booked August solid with these gigs if I wasn't doing Edinburgh.

The celebrities these five groups chose to star in my demonstration strip were Lionel Messi, Kim Kardashian, Michael Jackson, Bear Grylls, and, most original of the week, Bob Ross.

Sunday, 29 July 2018
Bob, My Gran & Guinea Pigs - comics by kids

My mega marathon tour of the north with my Comic Art Masterclass continued this week taking me, in one day, to Hartlepool and Stockton. It was inevitable that Hartlepool's comic would have Hangus The Monkey in - their most enduring legend. Meanwhile Stockton's cover has a drawing of a toy husky that one of the kids had with her.

The lovely market town of Leyburn in North Yorkshire played host to me for two sold out classes. This Summer Reading Challenge, of which all these classes have been part, does seem to be working as a project to get kids into the various libraries. Hopefully it will keep them coming.

To be honest I don't know why I bother inserting these Adsense adverts into my blogs. They upset the flow, and do you know how much I earn from them? In the last seven days - 1p, this month 3p. There is almost literally nothing I could do that would earn me less money that putting Adsense adverts in my blogs. What do you say? Should I stop?

The final day of the marathon saw me at Wollaton and Sherwood libraries in Nottinghamshire, making one of my favourite covers out of Bob. I'm particularly pleased by the way I got David Attenborough's name onto the cover. You are all aware that I include in every cover a reference to the celebrity the kids have chosen to appear in my demonstration strip? Good. Just making sure these details aren't wasted on you all.

I've had a chance to produce a few nifty flipcharts at most of these libraries. It really is a matter of how far in advance I can get into the room, and how much other setting up there is to do. Clearly Stockton and Hartlepool had done all the table-shifting to my satisfaction before I arrived.

The celebrities these six groups chose to star in my demonstration strip were Usain Bolt, Tom Cruise, The Queen, David Attenborough (twice), and Chris Pratt.

Tuesday, 31 July 2018
Hartlepool to home to Edinburgh -
travels with my art

Blimey, is that enough driving for
you? Check out these two Google
Maps, plotting my trip from home
on Tuesday morning to Worcester,
then to Darlington, Hartlepool,
Stockton, Leyburn then (cos you
couldn't fit that many destinations
on one Google Map) to
Nottingham, Kibworth, Derby,
Sheffield, home again, and straight
off the next morning all the way to
Edinburgh, where we'll be for the
next month.

I didn't bother including the map for
Monday's trip to Barnet and back,
and the preceding weekend's flight
and drive to Enniskillen and home.
But add those on and you can see
I've spent 10 solid days travelling,

of which more than 24 hours were
spent behind the wheel of a car. If
I've ever earned my Edinburgh
rest, of not having to drive for a
month, I've earned it this year.

In fact I will be driving a little bit,
with schools to do, and who knows
what other eventualities might
occur, but hopefully for most of the
next 27 days my car will be parked
up a long walk away, and I'll get
healthy with a lot of traipsing the
streets of Embra.

I could certainly do to lose some
weight. The big curse of travelling
is eating unhealthily. I try to do
better, but grabbing sandwiches at
lunch, being unable to resist a hotel
breakfast, and catering for myself
in the evening means I'm inevitably
eating less well than one does at
home. I've gulped down a few

slices of raw garlic in my hotel room, but it's not as easy to do as when you're in your kitchen. And there's something about shop-bought food that's more salty and sugary and less fresh than what your body needs. I talked to a comedian not long ago who's developed gout and put it down to Ginsters pasties. So, let's see if a month of flying and eating in our lovely new Edinburgh flat works its wonders.

Any big observations from my trip (which was, of course, to do a string of Comic Art Masterclasses which are well documented here)? Well Hartlepool is pretty run down, with a lot of effort being made to try and boost it, but with a lot of work to do. They have Wesleyan chapel whose roof is burnt out and that you can see ,from the neon Carling

sign out front, spent its last days as a night club. Called The Wesleyan. It's what he would have wanted.

Stockton On Tees is less run down, and included this Georgian looking building, with thick cobwebs in the window making it look like it's been empty for 50 years, but panning up to the sign you can see it was a wine bar until quite recently.

I stayed in The George Hotel in Piercebridge, which is where the song My Grandfathers Clock was written, and was in the pretty market town of Leyburn in North Yorkshire when the rains finally came, ending the two months of blazing sun, most of which has been happening while I've been indoors doing classes, or sat in a chilly air-conditioned car.

Wednesday, 1 August 2018
Posters and flyers, Edinburgh
begins

Big enough poster for you? This
year we've invested in some
slightly bigger posters. Not many,
three in fact. This one (a 60" x 40")
is the biggest, and the other two
are Quad posters which I haven't
found yet. But I felt I had to dip my
foot into the water and see if it
made any difference at all.

When you spot your big poster,
and take your photo with it, you feel
like you're such a big deal and it's

going to make such an impact.
What this photo doesn't show is me
pulling back to reveal the 10,000
other posters, all much bigger than
this, which have become the
modern posterised landscape of
Edinburgh.

We've come a long way since the
Socks' first year when a company
called Diabolical Liberties would
flypost your A2 posters all over the
city under cover of the night. Now
Bristol's own Out Of Hand have the
exclusive licence with the council to
provide and put up these vinyl
printed banners all over the city.
Given that our wee 60 x 40 costs
150 quid, and the two Quads cost
that much for two, I can't begin to
calculate how much has been
spent by other shows on their
posters. There are some shows for
which I've already walked past half

a dozen 8-foot-high banners, which must cost £250 a pop, and I know that's only the tip of their promotional iceberg. Shows must be spending tens of thousands on publicity, for shows in venues as small as mine where, as far as I can work out, you can't possibly earn those tens of thousands back in ticket sales. I'm sure they know what they're doing.

Me, I put my faith in the good old fashioned flyer. They arrived Tuesday, three boxes containing 10,000 flyers, which I shall be distributing personally on the streets of Edinburgh with my characteristic flick (see above). In fact I gave my first flick, not for my own flyer, but for the cast of a show who caught me on the street yesterday. They're called Strictly Arts and their show is called Freeman. Here's that first-flick-of-the-season in full...

Having arrived Monday afternoon I've already delivered t-shirts and comics to the Gilded Balloon shop, said hello to everyone at the venue and picked up my lanyard, done the long walk and parked the car (until Saturday when I'll be taking it out to do a class in a library), done my soundcheck and met my new tech Cassandra and found that Steve Gunn, my tech from last time, is now Head Of Production, and spent the day looking after Heather, who was suffering a severe allergic reaction to something so we had to phone NHS direct, get some medicine, oh it was all go (she's feeling better today).

All that and I got along to my first party. The first, and only, party I'll be able to go to and take advantage of the free drinks, in this case a Gin & Raspberry concoction. I met some nice people

Edinburgh Evening News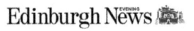

27 great shows to see at the Edinburgh Festival

August 20

Scottish Falsetto Sock Puppet Theatre: Superheroes

The Fringe veterans are back to stick their toes into the water of the world of superheroes and villains. Did you know DC Comics has a killer sock called Argh!Yle!? They probably do. Gilded Balloon Teviot, 10.30pm, £8.50/£10.50

- a couple who are producing and performing a show of the songs of Tom Waits & Leonard Cohen, a guy whose flatmate books the acts for the venue we were in, and Svetlana of Kev & Svetlana, with whom I talked Russia and politics. Some good drag acts, mixed with some camp acts, and a couple of cabaret acts with a camp/draggy crossover flavour. I believe they call it Variety. (I jest, I was really enjoying them, especially Myrna DuBois who is reminiscent of Lily Savage in her prime). I didn't stay late, leaving at a time before what will, starting tonight, be curtain up for my show. I really must adjust to Edinburgh time soon.

Show opens tonight, and I have a three minute slot on Chortle Fast Fringe before that. Best get stuck into the day. In the meantime, do enjoy a shot of our lovely flat. Better than we were expecting.

"Great show" - Edinburgh Evening News

Check this out from tonight's Edinburgh Evening News. We're one of their...

27 great shows to see at the Edinburgh Festival

August 20 **Scottish Falsetto Sock Puppet Theatre: Superheroes**
The Fringe veterans are back to stick their toes into the water of the world of superheroes and villains. Did you know DC Comics has a killer sock called Argh!Yle!? They probably do. Gilded Balloon Teviot, 10.30pm, £8.50/£10.50

Thursday, 2 August 2018
Fab first night in rainy Edinburgh

Here, in the window of the Gilded Balloon shop, we have the Socks' merchandise on sale. The Socks comic and t-shirts are waiting for the punters to snap them up, another first time venture for us. For reasons I can't fathom, I've never got our shirts into the shop before, only ever managing to sell them face to face. Well now you can buy them when you pick up your tickets, and I hope you all do.

The Socks' first night was a stonker, though we come away with one big lesson - the show's too long. Again. This happens every year. We write an hour long show, getting it down to approximately 60 minutes in previews, then it grows in Edinburgh, with audience laughter and ad libs, meaning we need to trim it. A good 5 minutes has to go from the current show. On our opening night we'd reached the 59 minute mark and hadn't even sung the final "reuniting" song, let alone done the finale. If it's any consolation, first night audience, the finale's not the best bit of the show, but we feel you were robbed. So, today some judicious trimming is underway.

Before our own show, The Socks made an appearance at Chortle's Fast Fringe, which was excellent. We were the 9th act on a bill of a dozen acts, each doing 3 minutes, and for the first half of the show the audience was taking a lot of warming up. It's a difficult show to keep the momentum going in, with such a variety of acts coming on an such breakneck speed. But by the time we came on they were more than ready and we absolutely killed.

We were blessed with a lovely bit of audience interaction.

Right Sock: Name a superhero, they might be in the show
Punter: Superman
Right Sock: Or they might not
(Audience laughter)
Punter (repeats): Superman
Right Sock: No, we heard you. I

the guest set needs mending. The cross bar is only held on by elastic bands, and has been ever since I lost one of fixing bolts during a gig on the Gilded Garden's outside stage (don't look for it, it's not there any more) in 2012. I must find a way of making it more secure, otherwise I can't lift the set with one hand, which makes getting on and off stage really hard.

don't know if you saw, we just did a gag that some might call witty, even ironic, based on the fact that we'd heard you and the audience heard us hearing you. By saying 'Superman' again you are, if anything, wasting time that we can't spare in this Three Minute Slot!

It doesn't read like anything, and the words will have been slightly different, but the timing was lovely and got great laughs from the knowledge that we were wasting a bit of our 3 minute slot talking about how we were wasting a bit of our 3 minute slot. Ah, you had to be there.

We then gave them Harley Quinn and Poison Ivy, which went brilliantly, and off to great applause. Some good exit flyering afterwards and, hopefully, that'll spread the word that our show's a laugh.

More notes that need working on:

Last night's opening audience, for our main show, wasn't bad. It beat 6 out of 9 shows, beating all of the "Modern Era" shows except 2015's Minging Detectives. Somehow, since our 2012 return, we've never managed the feat of '09 and '10 when our opening nights were sellouts. It was the past, they did things differently then.

And it's raining. We're all very nostalgic for the legendary summer of 2018 - do you remember it? When the sun shone all day, we reached record temperatures, and no-one thought it would ever end? That seems like years ago. I'm wearing an anorak and my flyers are sticking together. Onwards and upwards.

Dear reader, I am among that number.

Because of my religious regime of consuming slices of raw garlic washed down with orange juice every day, I seek normally to protect myself from this ailment. But by midday Thursday - Day 2 of my show - I had a sore throat and realised I had succumbed to something.

Friday, 3 August 2018
Edinburgh cold? Already? (Day 3)

There is a legendary disease they speak of in the ancient annals of that mysterious ceremony called the Edinburgh Fringe, known as The Edinburgh Cold.

With mind-numbing inevitability, a host of comedians - who have spent every night breathing the air of 50 or more strange people in a hot, humid, airless room, and shaking hands, air-kissing and giving each other bear hugs in the streets, at launch parties, and into the early hours in equally packed bars, and, in some cases, handing hundreds of flyers out to the great unwashed on the streets of the city - are suddenly surprised to find they've picked up some germs.

I managed the second night of my show fine, though they were a funny crowd who seemed not to get a lot of gags, and who laughed most at things like the bloke in the back row who kept shouting out the names of random superheroes (to be honest that was very funny, but it slightly derailed the rest of the hour. We finished on time though, so the day's editing had paid off in shortening the show).

This morning, Friday aka Day 3, I wake to find the Socks Voice is currently frayed. It has a reedy, two-pronged sound to it, which is not a good thing. I will have to spend the day nursing that voice and being kind to myself. That or we'll be doing our first Friday night show as a mime.

It could be worse, I could be doing a Comic Art Masterclass in the daytime tomorrow as well as hoping for a sellout show that night.

In other news, at yesterday's Gilded Balloon launch party I learned that the reason there aren't so many big name TV comedians at Edinburgh this year is that they've all been playing at the Just For Laughs Festival. They have, apparently, been going there because that's where Netflix are going to shop for talent, and they're not coming to Edinburgh. So if you're angling for a TV special, you do a week in Canada instead of a month in Edinburgh. Where the biggest thing you're going to pick up is strep throat.

Colds, clogged drains, and cancellations - a tough first week

This has been an unexpectedly challenging first week at the Fringe. Definitely the most problematic week since 2009 (when we woke up to an early phone call from home telling us our flat had been entirely flooded out by a leak from upstairs, a disaster that took till the end of the year to repair, and which we've never quite got over). So far no ceilings have fallen in, as far as we know, but if they were to, this would be the year they'd choose to do it.

We started with Hev having a severe allergic reaction to whatever she ate on the journey up, or on the first day here. Her throat was swollen and she was shivering and shuddering in the most worrying way. Calls to NHS Direct and visits to pharmacists found us Piriton, Kalms, and various things that are helping in a small way, but we still have ongoing problems with what Hev can eat these days. She's worried one of the things she could be allergic to is sunflowers - having bought some to decorate the flat, and cooked our first meal in sunflower oil rather than our usual extra virgin - so I had to take the clutch of sunflowers out of the flat and resdistribute them. You'll probably still spot a few in odd places around the Royal Mile/St Marys Street area (hence the photo above).

Talking of changing the subject, the plumbing was blocked so we had to get a man in. When we arrived in the flat it had a pooey smell emanating from the kitchen, which cleared up after a bit of use. But then we found the sink wouldn't drain, and when the washing machine emptied, it emptied up through the sink. I found myself scooping buckets of water from the filling sink and chucking them out of the window. Luckily it's been raining for the first three days we've been here, so nobody noticed. A quick visit by the plumber sorted that one.

Then on day two of my show I've managed to get a cold, The Edinburgh Cold. I could feel it burning around the back of my throat on Thursday and on Friday I was fully colded-up and in danger of losing my voice. By taking it easy on the flyering* - which I can't do silently, try as I might - and by treating my throat carefully and doing warming up exercises in the falsetto voice all the way to performance time, I got through and had a great show on Friday (day 3).

Saturday was always going to be harder for the voice because, during the day, I'd lined up a Comic Art Masterclass at Meadowbank Library near Falkirk. I did that, and it went well, but I could feel the toll being taken on the voice. Never forgetting that date last year at the

Bill Murray where I had to cancel the gig - first time ever - I knew I had to avoid over-exertion or I could totally wipe out my performing voice. But it was Saturday, and if I didn't flyer hard I wasn't going to get a sellout. We always get a sellout on the first Saturday, without fail**.

Reader, this year we failed. I simply couldn't spend as many hours flyering as was needed (I did about two and a half hours in all), and critically I couldn't do the hour in the run up to the show, when I usually breeze round the tables in the bar outside the venue reminding everyone that our show's starting soon. That always whips up a good few stragglers, but it also uses the wrong part of my voice box. And from 7.30 till the start of my show at 10.30 I was having to speak, or try to, entirely in the falsetto voice.

I say speak. At 7.30 I had only a whisper coming out, and my falsetto voice was a wheezy croak. Never before have I had to coax a voice out from such an unpromising start. But by golly I did it, and am pretty bloody proud of myself. Our audience may have been our lowest first Saturday since 2013** , but the voice held up throughout. During the show The Socks didn't even mention the lost voice situation, which we had done the previous night, and the audience were none the wiser and had a great show. I think there were reviewers in that night. So, if they give us poor reviews, and we drop down a star or two, I'll just be able to smile silently to myself in the knowledge that they were watching an act that, three hours earlier, had no bloody voice. So there.

(At time of typing, 8.30 Sunday morning, I have no voice again, having done nothing more than whisper so far. And, of course, the cold has moved on to the tickly cough stage. So let us look forward to a repeat performance of the threatened performance again tonight).

So we've had colds, we've had clogs, but now, for the first time we have cancellations.

For the first time ever at the Fringe I'm cancelling shows, on Wednesday and Thursday, because I have to fly down to England to see Mum. She's been deteriorating over recent weeks and at the end of the week had another of a succession of falls which has meant her going into hospital and realising she's not going to be going back home. As she said, when we spoke on the phone on Saturday morning, "it's time to put our plans into operation". So, though hopefully she could have a long time ahead of her, she wants to see us and get her affairs in order while she's still compos mentis (the cancer now having spread to her brain) and that's what I'll be doing in the middle of the week. Jude, who's been on holiday in Spain for the last two weeks, has been dealing with more of it than I have, long distance, and goes to see Mum today (Sunday).

Obviously the Mum situation hangs over everything, and has been the biggest concern, with Jude, Hev and I knowing we couldn't have picked worse times to be in other countries. But it couldn't be helped. I'm glad I was able to visit Mum in Kibworth last week (blimey, it was literally only seven days ago, it feels like an age) and help her in the small ways I could. Let's see what else I can do this week. Two shows cancelled, but hopefully the punters will come on another day (there are also 4 comps issued on those days, which are bound to be reviewers, fingers crossed they'll reschedule), and I've had to cancel, or hopefully move, a comic class too.

Doing the Edinburgh Fringe makes us all a bit self-obsessed, so I apologise for this maudlin indulgent screed when so many people have so many worse problems going on in their lives. As it is, we're both quite cheerful up here, and the Socks have been having great shows with fabulous audiences. Onwards and upwards, it's Sunday and I need to sprook tonight's show for all I'm worth.

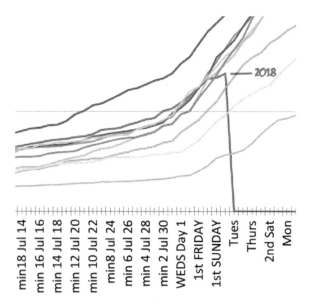

min18 Jul 14 · min 16 Jul 16 · min 14 Jul 18 · min 12 Jul 20 · min 10 Jul 22 · min8 Jul 24 · min 6 Jul 26 · min 4 Jul 28 · min 2 Jul 30 · WEDS Day 1 · 1st FRIDAY · 1st SUNDAY · Tues · Thurs · 2nd Sat · Mon

— 2018

Monday, 6 August 2018
Flatlining - Is this the year that Flyering stopped working?

Look at that graph. Isn't that the most miserable thing you ever saw? Probably not, cos it's not your show. But having had to cancel two shows (for family reasons, going to England for 2 days) my sales line temporarily nosedived as people got their money back. And then today's uptick? Well, it simply doesn't compare with previous years.

Could this be the year when flyering stopped working?

When I took my first show to the Edinburgh Fringe, The Sitcom

Trials way back in 2001, I discovered how flyering worked. More precisely I discovered that flyering did work.

It was a revelation to me to find the streets were full of punters, all in town in order to see shows, and all you had to do was persuade them that yours was the show they wanted. That year's show had a breakeven of 30 punters per day, and I found that three hours of flyering would bring in the said thirty bums on seats.

This became known, if only by me, as Kev F's Theory Of Flyering. 3 hours of flyering equalled 30 bums on seats. As recently as 2015 I tested it out under laboratory conditions (okay, I recorded a couple of days flyering and leaped to some vague conclusions), and it seemed that the theory still held true.

That very first flyer, from 2001. (An overstickered version, cos we had lots left over. That year I also discovered you only need 10,000 flyers, and I'd printed 25,000.)

I also demonstrated how not flyering would lower sales when, in 2002 and 2012, I made the same mistake twice. I did two shows a day. And, since I have always been single-handedly responsible for my own promotion, I was able to do half as much flyering per show and, lo, each show sold half as well as previously.

But this year I'm struggling. Today, for example, I've done nearly four hours of flyering and my sales for tonight - on 2 for 1 day, which I've sold out almost every year - are stuck on 53 (a sellout being 90). They were 53 before I'd given out a single flyer and they're fifty bloody three after two bursts of pretty bloody good flyering.

My technique remains the best. Everyone gets The Snap, they get the smile, they get a witty sales line

(be it "this is what you're looking for", "they're on at 10.30", "they're selling out but you might squeeze in tonight" etc), and they take the flyer. More people take my flyers than take anyone else's flyers. I see it all day every day, and it's been a source of pride for the last 18 years.

Except that in all those previous years the proof of the pudding was in the eating, and this year it's not. The flyers aren't turning into ticket sales.

Maybe it's my mood - I am exhausted with the cold, and with having to cancel two shows to go down and see Mum, and the whole Mum situation is obviously very depressing - but I feel like I've never before encountered so many resistant punters. The Royal Mile has always been a bit of a waste of time, with such a high proportion of tourists being Tattooies and day-trippers, who don't even know the Fringe exists and have no intention of going to any show of any sort even if they did. There have always been lots of Tattooies, but their lot was usually leavened by the Fringegoers who would coalesce around the Fringe Office box office queue. That queue is now a distant memory.

With the growth of online ticket buying, and the profusion of cross-venue box offices (for example the Underbelly, Gilded Balloon, Pleasance & Assembly all sell each others tickets), there is now no reason for the queue at the Fringe Office to be a focus any more. It used to be the greatest place to flyer. A few years ago, when everyone started flyering the queue (something which had once being the province of a small few of us) the stewards cracked down on it. But you could always spot the likely punters on their way there. Now you can't.

My flyering strip of choice is the stretch around the Gilded Balloon, where there is a healthy flow of punters. But two factors have made that less effective year on year. One is the profusion of other flyerers - there are more than I have ever seen along that stretch. The other is the resistant punters. I feel like I have been told "no thanks" more than ever. There are more people going past who have already bought their tickets for another show, or aren't going to any shows anywhere.

I have a feeling that more people have decided what they're going to see before they get here - as recorded last week, I had near-record high pre-sales before we arrived in Edinburgh - and they're less susceptible to being whipped into my show by me and my bits of cardboard. Could it be that the battle is won, by all those shows with big agencies whose PRs have got them coverage in the national press months ago, long before August starts? I also have paranoid doubts that people may be looking at the flyer and thinking it's a kids show (I was warned against having cartoons on the flyer for this very reason, back in the spring). Or am I simply losing the race to other more attractive acts? Sorry, it's possible to get very maudlin and introspective when you let Edinburgh get to you, and it rather looks like I've let it get to me this week. (And my god is there anything more depressing than a Sold Out board that's packed with act after act, and you're not on it? I'm making myself more miserable by thinking these things out loud).

I will continue with my tried and tested method of old. But if my experience of this past few days continues, and I am incapable of getting good sized audiences into my room on a regular basis, then I will have to reconsider this promotional method in future. Let's be honest, I'm not getting any younger and it's knackering!

Oh yes, and those bloody posters that I paid extra for have done bugger all. I haven't even seen the damn things yet! Mental note: Do not spend money on big posters in future.

(It's an hour later than when I started this blog. I check back on my sales. It's 8.35pm and they've crept up to… 53)

UPDATE: In the end, sales of Monday's show ended up at 63*, after two minutes of last minute "they start soon" flyering. Could it be that was the most effective flyering of the day?

Tuesday, 7 August 2018
Benedict Cumberbatch Stole My Act - Chortle

This, on Chortle, as part of their Big Ask questionnaire: (read the other comedians' much funnier answers here)

Benedict Cumberbatch stole my act... literally!

The Big Ask: Who is the best person you've met at the Fringe?

Benedict Cumberbatch. He stole the Socks. At the bar of the Gilded Balloon he inadvertently started walking off with the bag that had the moist and smelly post-show Sock puppets in, thinking it was his friend's. Had a very enjoyable half hour chat with pre-fame 'call me Ben'.**Scottish Falsetto Sock Puppet Theatre, Scottish Falsetto Sock Puppet Theatre: Superheroes, Gilded Balloon, 22:30**

Wednesday, 8 August 2018
The Fall & Rise Of The Voice -
Show survives Edinburgh cold

Wow, I even managed to take a Sock selfie before the show, the first time there's been time for that in the frantic 15 minute handover all week.

After the miserable diatribe yesterday, this is just a quick post to say I have cheered up. It was the cold, the common cold that is, that was making me excessively depressed and casting a shadow over my view of the world.

My shows have been hard to do with the croaky, and almost nonexistent, voice caused by the cold. It's been:

Weds (Day 1) - fine and fab

Thurs (Day 2) - fine, but starting to feel burning around throat
Friday (Day 3) - swollen throat, hard to swallow. Groggy with cold, lots of sleeps. Performed fine

Sat - Class during day, strained voice. Voiceless at 7.30, nursed voice carefully, it held out through show beautifully
Sun - Voiceless through day, again nursed voice carefully, meaning less flyering, show went perfectly

Mon - Thought voice would be okay, as it had come back during the day. But by night the falsetto was still "split" and reedy. This was the hardest show to do, almost inaudible at times. I was very drained and depressed afterwards.

Tues - thought voice was okay, started fine, but got weaker as show progressed, croaking by the end

So I'm grateful in part for these two days off to go and see Mum, as it will serve the secondary purpose of letting my voice recover. And can I say a special thanks to the act I hand over to after my show, Grant Buse, who has introduced me to a fantastic thing called Singer Spray. I've only had a couple of scooshes of it, administered by Grant before my shows, but it was what enabled me (and the Socks) to hold out for half of Tuesday night's show. He's been in Avenue Q, so he knows a bit about preserving a falsetto voice. Thanks Grant.

If anybody saw the problem shows from Saturday to Tuesday, and thank god I didn't record any of them, you might have spotted that the cold affects certain parts of my falsetto range. So on Saturday and Sunday, though I was able to articulate words clearly, there were bits of songs that I had to change the key of or speak.

For example in the **Avengers Reel**, a medley of seven different songs all in different keys (a version of which you can see here*) the Socks have to reach some quite low notes (low for them, normal for a regular voice) and those are the notes that the cold choked off most. Come the second halves of Monday & Tuesdays shows, most singing notes had become pretty feeble.

When we return on Saturday, I aim to be in full voice. And, you never know, we might capture something on camera.

Wednesday, 8 August 2018

"One of the guiltiest pleasures you'll find at the Fringe" - Scottish Daily Mail

This lovely box out review/preview is in today's Scottish Daily Mail. How about that? Hev spotted it first online, and then we went out and found it in print. Thankyou the Scottish Daily Mail, we look forward to that boosting our numbers and no mistake.

SCOTTISH FALSETTO SOCK PUPPET THEATRE: SUPERHEROES *Scottish Daily Mail 8 Aug 2018* THERE are some incredibly talented, internationally renowned puppet theatre companies to be found at the Fringe, but to my mind you can't beat this dose of homegrown

IO ƏUO

comedy. The socks' profane, hilarious and ribald shows have previously tackled Shakespeare and space, minging detectives and even the Socky Horror Show. Now, the focus is on superheroes, making this a surefire cult hit – and one of the guiltiest pleasures you'll find at the Fringe. Will you laugh your socks off?

Gilded Ballon Teviot, until Aug 26 (sic)

Saturday, 11 August 2018
Looking After Mum - 2 days away
Mum visiting Hev and me in Edinburgh in 2016

On Wednesday morning I flew down to East Midlands airport and took Earth's cheapest hire car (£12, about which later) to Kibworth, to join Jude in looking after Mum.

I cancelled two nights of shows in Edinburgh, for the first time, because of the ominous sounding news about Mum that came in last weekend. She'd had another fall, which it turned out was one of four last week. This time she was taken to hospital, and this time Mum was pretty sure she didn't want to go back to Windmill Gardens.

As the most recent prognosis showed that the cancer has spread to her brain, and thought the recent course of radiotherapy had only finished the previous Monday, it was clear her condition wasn't getting any better. Dizziness has caused earlier falls, and now it was physical weakness that was to blame. She is having too much difficulty walking, and even getting in and out of bed, to be left unattended. And so, while she is

care home visits for Thursday.

Jude has been magnificent, doing far much more in this process than I've available to do, and possibly capable of. The arranging of the care workers who've been tending to Mum at home for the past month or so has all been Jude's doing. And though I've taken on Power Of A Turkey (it's what we call it, allow us our moments of levity) and taken charge of the money for funeral arrangements, Jude's sorted out the paying of the bills so far. Her job is such that she's able to work away from the office for great lengths of time, and has been spending every night in Kibbie going through mountains of email in her role as Whatever The Hell It Is She Does at Ealing Council. (She must have told me 50 times by now, it genuinely never sticks).

physically alert and totally compos mentis (a phrase that, can I just say, autocorrect will not tolerate, whatever device I'm writing on! Mum has been composed mantis and compost mentos in recent messages), she's ready to go into a care home.

So, while the first half of Wednesday was spent with Jude and Mum waiting for an ambulance to take them from the Royal Infirmary in Leicester to St Luke's cottage hospital in Harborough, and me getting on with work at Windmill Gardens (I script edited the show, changing the running order to great and successful effect), the later afternoon saw us getting Mum settled in at St Lukes, and discussing with nurses and various practitioners what our options were. We lined up three

Mum visiting her alma mater Edinburgh College Of Art, for the first time in 60 years, August 2016

Thursday morning we went to visit Mum, who's sleepy and wanting rest, but is her normal mentally alert self beneath the sluggishness. We learned more about the difference between CHC and FNC (forms of care funding, neither of

(easy) or the Hudl (nightmare and with less capacity than a wristwatch) and can take it to somewhere with wifi to download more show for her, she'll just settle for the TV in the room, which she's sharing with an equally quiet women of a similar vintage.

I realise I've devoted more column inches to Mum's TV viewing than her medical condition. Which is how it should be. We're all three of us quite resigned to the inevitability of the situation and frankly Mum doesn't want anyone going over and over it when you can't change anything. What we could do was sort out a nice place for her to stay.

And, hopefully, we've found it. Subject to an assessment next week, when they decide whether she's in the right state to go there (and everyone so far thinks she is), Mum should be going into Kibworth Knoll. We looked at three places of which the Knoll was by far the best. One, in Harborough, as a residential and nursing home, which was too clinical and more than Mum needs right now; and one, in Kibworth, was a bit of a joke, being run by a well-intentioned but not very professional couple who were

which Mum is sick enough to be eligible for now) and spent a lot of time just chatting. We did marginally well in providing Mum with TV shows to watch. She has a Hudl, a downmarket tablet thing which I find really hard to operate, onto which I downloaded an Eastenders and a Poldark (she watched the Eastenders and informed me "I don't like bloody Poldark"). I'd also brought with me my old iPhone 5s onto which I'd loaded two earlier Eastenders, a Casualty (which she watched), the movie Florence Foster Jenkins (which we left her watching on Thursday), and Poldark again (I didn't know at the time!). Unfortunately she has no wifi in St Lukes, so unless some kindly nurse has the time and the inclination, and can get their heads around the working of the iPhone

entertaining but not for us.

Implicated by Walter Tottle, performed by Nick, Kev and Noddy, written by me & Nick, filmed at The Knoll, 1981

The bonus about the Knoll is that it's where my childhood best mate Nick Tyson used to live. Between 1976 and 1983 I spent many a long hour there, from doing sleepovers and rehearsing with the band - our first rehearsal room The Mission Hut was in the garage building which is now a two storey house - to filming pop videos. In the low-tech classic Implicated (1981, above) you can see the central staircase, which is still there, and the main lounge which still survives, and glimpse the fifteen foot long stained glass skylight over the central balcony, most of which is now covered by suspended ceiling, the balcony converted into rooms and corridors. The back garden where we filmed half the video, and the video for Take The Wires Out(1982), has long since been built over by an extension as long as the original house, and more. So Mum's going to be living at Nick's, ain't that perfect?

Again, the second longest paragraph of this diary is about my old pop videos, rather than Mum. What can I say? You knew I was a shallow egoist before you took me in.

Mum's happy with the Knoll decision, which was ultimately hers, so while I scooted off home to Edinburgh, and Jude will be going back to the Family in London for the weekend, she'll be back on Monday to tend to Mum and the transfer, while I'm liaising long distance with various people. Now, did I mention I got a hire car for £12?

Now I know why Green Motion cars at East Midlands Airport are having to hire cars out at twelve quid a time. They are impossible to return the car to. Their office is at the

Hilton Hotel, a 10 minute drive from the airport. This was easy enough when I was picking it up, I was met by a man in a van at the airport. But on returning the car one suddenly finds that the roads are being rebuilt and, certainly in my case, satnav doesn't know where the new roads are. So the turning for the Hilton, which looks really clear and goes left off the M1, isn't there any more. After overshooting twice, I found myself in a panic at missing my flight, being talked-through on the phone by the poor guy at Green Motion, who's clearly having to do this with every other customer, then as soon as I dropped off, leaping into the waiting van to be driven to the airport. In future I shall pay the extra to ensure I get car hire which picks up and drops off at the airport. At least they sign-post airports when they move the roads.

Second longest paragraph again, all about me. I'd better stop now before we forget Mum is supposed to be the subject. Here, let's enjoy a few more photos of her visit to Edinburgh back in 2016.

Wednesday, 15 August 2018
Is Edinburgh Quieter This Year?

After two weeks, I've finally spotted one of our quad posters, on the far side of The Meadows facing away from the road. Still have yet to find the other poster.

Is Edinburgh Quieter This Year?

I've read nothing about the Fringe-going visitor population of Edinburgh being any lower than previous years, and I've not read any show complaining about low audience numbers. So, I've got to ask: is Edinburgh quieter this year?

I'll be the first to put my head above the parapet and say my audience numbers are lower than previous years and the streets look relatively quiet to me.

The Socks' Superheroes show is not doing badly, and by the standards of a lot of shows I know we're doing well. I know this anecdotally, from having seen the size of queues going into other shows in my building. But looking at my sales graph, which shows me the Scottish Falsetto Socks sales for every one of their 10 years of shows, I'm looking at

crowds that are just that bit smaller than before.

And it's not as if we're not going for them. Yesterday (Tuesday) I did the longest stint of flyering so far this year. The passing punters of Bristo Square got five hours of quality flyering from me. They were good (ie the sort of people who look like they go to comedy and theatre), they were receptive (they took the flyers and laughed and said thank you), they looked as likely to come to the show as any punters I've seen in my 18 years of Edinburgh flyering.

I even got to exit-flyer the audience of Chortle Fast Fringe where the Socks had just done a cracking three minute slot. You can't do better and more efficient flyering than I did on Tuesday 14th August.

But despite all that, Kev F's Theory Of Flyering failed to be borne out. My theory, established in 2001 and tested every year since, hypothesises that 3 hours of flyering will equate to 30 bums on seats. Celebratory blogs like this one from 2015 show me adding 100 sales in a day through intense flyering. Tuesday's 5 hours of flyering turned the morning's figure of 17 tickets sold to a final tally of just 36 tickets sold.

And it's not as if we could be suffering bad word-of-mouth. This year's show is in perfect shape now, with audiences laughing throughout and giving me great direct feedback. I know it's vain, and could be self-deluding, but I think you know when your show's good (for example, in 2015, I didn't feel my show, Minging Detectives, was the best, and in fact found myself apologising for it in conversations with fans a year later). This year I have no such doubts. Superheroes is a hilarious show, and songs like Bechdel Test, Avengers Reel and Dead Ringer For Superman deserve 4 star reviews on their own. But we've had no reviews yet, which can't be helping.

And we have crowds that, though lovely and voluble - and seemingly full, thanks to fellow performers getting in with their passes and filling up the back rows - just don't include as many paying customers as past years. Thanks to the double oddity of having to cancel two shows in week one for family reasons and flyering less in week one because of my cold, our sales graph is deceptively low. But if you close up the two-day flatline on the graph, total sales for 2018 are behind every year except for 07 (debut show) 08 (Return) and 12 (the notorious Olympic year). Remember, just three weeks ago, we were looking at record-breaking advance sales. Suggesting that our core punters are as strong as ever, it's the passing trade that's fallen off.

So, I put the question out there, is Edinburgh quieter this year? Is any other show, which has been here before, seeing smaller attendances than before? Is anyone feeling that the bars are quieter, the streets are emptier, and the punters are staying away?

Or, horror of horrors, is it just us?

UPDATE. 8pm, twelve hours later i've had lots of responses to this blog. As well as conversations on the street with three comedians and two reviewers, all of whom agreed that things were quiet this year, these Facebook comments came in. My further thoughts are below them.

Patricia Silver yes it seems quieter this year

Daphna Baram It is quiet for me but this is my first full run since 2015 and my venue is a bit off the beaten track.

James Worthington We felt last year was much quieter than most, especially than the year previous. Is it dying out?

Dave Flynn I'm a punter at the Fringe, who has been coming here since 2007. I've seen 25 shows so far this year, and I've never been to so many packed out venues before.

Steve Day I've not noticed it being quiet. The pavements seem, if anything, more thronged than I can remember. I've been delighted with my numbers.

James Cook Personal perspective from the 3 shows I do:
1. A kids show at 10:45am - never done one before. Smallest crowd has been 3 families, biggest about 15. Increase on previous years - infinity per cent.
2. Board Game Smackdown. 3rd fringe in the biggest venue yet (100 cap) not uncommon for us to have standing room only and have had to turn people away a handful of times. Increase on previous years: easily 50%
3. A stand up show. Only the second non themed show I've done. Had 11 in last night and was disappointed - two years ago I would have been happy with that. Have been getting around 25, 50 at weekends.

Paul Savage Defo quieter.

Mill Goble Definitely quieter on the

press front, and when flyering 12-1, 85% of the people I see are other folk doing shows or Spanish tourists. Of the five or so shows I've seen, they've probably been averaging about 35-50% full.

Lindsey Marie Silver There are more meeting places/watering holes this year. I think that's why it feels quieter out and about.

Alex Petty I've not noticed it being quieter. cowgate is heaving and even more dangerous to pedestrians than ever, the mile is packed and venues are reporting increased takings - though a small increase rather than a giant leap. Show numbers around my venues seem to be good overall too from reports I've had.

Paul Currie It is apparently

according to the taxi drivers .. and they know

Ewan Leeming Anecdotally:

1/ We're printing a lot more than usual - especially more flyers which generally means people let down by big companies or making last minute change of plans.

2/ Performers in central venues generally saying bigger audiences.

3/ Performers in less central areas generally saying lower audiences.

4/ Niche acts reporting bigger audiences.

Anthony Jeannot Nothing to compare it to, so not super helpful, but in a very small venue, I did not need to flyer this year and had it 70-100% full right through the run. In my first run, if this is what it's like in a down year, I'd love to see it at full tilt.

Andre Vincent (on an independent thread):
The Voodoo Rooms are not getting the traffic it used to get and they need bums on seats.

Pete Harris My experience this year is an noticeable increase in punters, probably, in part, to do with the good weather in the first

two weeks.

So, my further thoughts? The people above who are happy with their numbers, eg James, Steve, Alex are in Free Fringe venues (though others, eg Voodoo Rooms, in FF are struggling). Could it be that what punters there are will take a punt on free, but not on paid?

My new theory, conjured up this afternoon, is that a new generation of millennial punters may be used to the concept of "A Festival" as a thing you pay to go to, where you meet friends, you hang out and eat and drink, and you'll watch acts performing for free - a la Glastonbury, Latitude etc - but you don't think of paying money in advance to watch an act.

Whereas, once upon a time, people went to the Edinburgh Festival Fringe to watch a range of theatre, art and comedy, they now to go Edinburgh to "be at a Festival". But the seven-shows-a-day punter, with their tightly planned schedule and their deep pockets willing to take a punt on seeing something they've never heard of before, is an ancient beast on the brink of extinction.

Look at Bristo Square & George Square. Hundreds of people are sat at tables, drinking beer and coffee, and eating at a bigger range of street food stalls than ever before - just like they did the previous month at Latitude, Reading and Larmer Tree (is it any coincidence that all those open areas now have mock grass flooring to resemble a Festival in a field?). If someone had come up to them at one of those field-festivals waving a flyer asking them to pay an extra ten quid to sit inside and be performed at for an hour they'd have thought you were mental. Why, they ask quite reasonably, are these Edinburgh nutters breaking the rules of Festivals by doing it here?

So that's my follow up question. Have Festivals ruined the Fringe?

Wednesday, 15 August 2018
Wonderful World

Just for you, a brand new clip from the Scottish Falsetto Socks' new Edinburgh show, Superheroes - What A Wonderful World, in which the Socks sing about the sort of Batman and Superman film they'd make.

More clips from the show will find their way online soon, though at time of writing we don't have a complete recording of the show yet (my batteries ran out halfway through, may need a new battery).

Thursday, 16 August 2018
Packing Tape Man

A brand new clip from last night's Scottish Falsetto Socks: Superheroes show, when the audience suggested Packing Tape Man, and the boys had to make of it what they could. Relax kids, the rest of the show is very tightly scripted, honest.

SCOTTISH FALSETTO SOCK PUPPET THEATRE: SUPERHEROES

Michael Flett | August 16, 2018 | Theatre | No Comments

They have become something of a Fringe institution, or perhaps they just require institutionalised, the antics of the Scottish Falsetto Sock Puppet Theatre returning to the Gilded Balloon for a tenth season, this year with a show entitled *Superheroes*, with no expense spared* as the greatest heroes and villains of Marvel and DC arrive in the form of knitted cotton.

A sold-out late slot on a Saturday night, the presence of puppets does not indicate that this is a show suitable for children, an on this occasion due to some unfeasibly uncooperative props there is perhaps even more profanity than usual in the ad-libbing, often as hilarious as the scripted gags.

Friday, 17 August 2018

"One of the most entertaining and anarchic nights out in the Fringe" - Geek Chocolate

Thanks to the lovely Michael Flett at Geek Chocolate for our first review of the Fringe! And a smasher it is too. They don't give stars, but darned if those don't read as a four.

SCOTTISH FALSETTO SOCK PUPPET THEATRE: SUPERHEROES

They have become something of a Fringe institution, or perhaps they just require institutionalised, the antics of the Scottish Falsetto Sock Puppet Theatre returning to the Gilded Balloon for a tenth season, this year with a show entitled *Superheroes*, with no expense spared* as the greatest heroes and villains of Marvel and DC arrive in the form of knitted cotton.

A sold-out late slot on a Saturday night, the presence of puppets does not indicate that this is a show suitable for children, an on this occasion due to some unfeasibly uncooperative props there is perhaps even more profanity than usual in the ad-libbing, often as hilarious as the scripted gags.

Featuring a better Joker than Jared Leto, the show is also educational, enlightening the audience to the meaning of motion capture (for those who think they already know; you're wrong) and the differences between cosmopolitan, Neapolitan and neo-classical, though the songs are largely reworkings of classic pop.

What might be more obscure to some is the Bechdel Test and the importance of modern entertainment to embrace its challenge, and thanks to a guest appearance by Harley Quinn and Poison Ivy discussing something other than their shared nemesis "with pointed ears who wears his pants on the outside – it's not exactly Dostoyevsky," it could be argued that *Superheroes* passes. Supported by Cassie the Technician who provides the varied musical accompaniment, the terrible puns are fast and land with a suitable kapow, for certainly the audience were groaning, and while a knowledge of Scots dialect and superhero lore is helpful to get the most out of the show the antics and shenanigans are sufficiently lively to carry the uninitiated through the maelstrom.

The current profile of superheroes higher than it has ever been thanks to the recent offerings of DC and Marvel such as *Justice League* and *Infinity War*, these are of course addressed, but nor are the classics forgotten, the trailblazing performances of Adam West, Lynda Carter and Christopher Reeve, all celebrated in one of the most entertaining and anarchic nights out in the Fringe.

Superheroes continues until Sunday 26th August

*taking into account Fringe ticket prices, the ongoing policy of austerity, pre-Brexit anxiety and the harsh rule of Thanos

Saturday, 18 August 2018
Superted vs Jimmy Savile

Another brand new clip from the Socks' Thursday night performance of Superheroes, this time they're ad-libbing about Superted and Jimmy Savile. Relax, some proper scripted stuff will eventually find its way online. Enjoy, if you can.

Saturday, 18 August 2018
Passing The Bechdel Test

A classic from the Scottish Falsetto Socks' show Superheroes - Passing The Bechdel Test. A song that I'm quite proud of, it's now online in both subtitled and vanilla form. Enjoy whichever you prefer.

There's also a big square version on Facebook, for your pleasure.

hope springs eternal that he & Claire might catch our show while they're up here.

Monday, 20 August 2018
Tortoise and Tweets - a half time report

Here we see the goodies from the goodie bag we all came away with after a pleasant afternoon soiree organised by Hare & Tortoise Productions, the new company set up by Jon Rolph & Claire Nosworthy. Jon, you won't remember, produced my BBC radio pilots Come Together and Meanwhile, way back in the days of yon and yore, and it was great to hear from him again. Having been producing the likes of Armstrong and Miller, and currently developing the Scarfolk Council into a TV series, he has bigger fish to fry than the little old Socks, though

The do started at 11am and, by dint of the fact that I was en route to the last of the month's Comic Art Masterclasses that afternoon, I was the first person to arrive. And it would seem the only performer in Edinburgh who was awake before midday. The goodie bag is the most Edinburgh-friendly you could conjure up, and the Lockets were immediately got through, along with the various energy food & drinks and, of course, the Tunnocks tea cake.

I've been Tweeting very heavily this Edinburgh season. Whether or not it's been to any avail, it is hard to say. Our numbers, as reported elsewhere, are down on previous years, but that is for myriad reasons, which will be investigated thoroughly at the end of the month.

Whether they've been bumped up or left totally unaffected by our Twitter activity I really cannot tell. They probably haven't been helped by these rather desperate tweets where, in bursts of passive-aggressive ennui, I've let it be known how hard I've found flyering, some days this month. There have been, it's felt, an inordinate number of resistant punters, in comparison to previous years. This could be faulty selective memory and bias confirmation, but there have been days when you wonder where I ever got that idea that the streets of Edinburgh were full of punters looking for shows to see, and all you had to do was convince them yours was the one they wanted.

There have been a few days when the flyering experience has reminded me of Adelaide. It was

there that we found everyone had "already got one". That meant either they'd already booked the one show they were going to see that night, or they already had a flyer and were limiting themselves. This year I've also found that an awful lot of people seem to be day trippers or folks on the final day of their holiday who, by the middle of the afternoon, are on their way home. This phenomenon occurs on any given day of the week, bizarrely.

And, with the exception of Geek Chocolate's lovely report, we haven't had a single review this year. Nothing with stars on, nothing from a familiar name. I have, with only 7 shows left, given up hope on getting any reviews which will be seen by punters and have, instead, just started Tweeting our old reviews from 2009 to 2016. Five stars from Edinburgh Evening News, 4 stars The Scotsman. Ah, memories.

NB: My blog about whether Edinburgh is quieter this year, has been read 880 times. Since which time we've just had the busiest weekend when nobody would be under the illusion that the city was in any way quiet. They were a lot of drunks and stag parties, the like of which nobody would want within a mile of their show, but there were certainly a lot of them, so yeah tourism.

Wednesday, 22 August 2018
That Night

Every Edinburgh run includes a night which becomes known as "That Night". A night when, assuming every other night has been going swimmingly and you're doing a show you're happy with, the audience will come along and simply not get it. It happened this week on Monday night when a healthily sized audience sat there in near silence, seeming to not understand gags, or maybe just dislike them. It's hard to tell, though I did hear one woman talking to a friend as they left asking "how much of that did you understand?". So quite possibly there was a contingent with English as a second language, we will never know.

You know That Night's gone badly when you get your only bad audience review. The edfringe.com website only has six reviews on it for the Socks, all glowing. Then someone called Keith D has come along, clearly on That Night, and provided the poo in the punchbowl. He writes "Very disappointing show. Avoid if you can. Part of the show was not even performed, as the 'sock puppets' ran out of time.

The only vaguely amusing bit was when the sock puppet 'outfits' started falling apart mid-act." (I thought it was Keith D, who I know on Facebook and who is notable misanthropic towards the Fringe in general, but he reports that it's not him, adding " I shall find this imposter and kill him with socks"). I am reminded of the two audiences that came to our Glasgow previews back in March, one of whom loved the show and one of whom was the "Hooray Henries" who sat there playing with their phones and soured the mood for everyone. Maybe they'd come back on Monday to wreak their revenge and repeat the experience?

I'm happy to report that Tuesday night's show was a return to form, and with only five performances left to go, even if we were to have another That Night every night, and let's hope we won't, it would remain statistically insignificant and won't sully the memory of an excellent show that's been a joy to perform almost every night.

And, as if to prove that no night is all bad, the video of Dead Ringer For Supermanthat has gone online was recorded on That Night. The laughter's not as big as the other two nights we got on camera, but the lyrics are clearer and the shots of the costume collapse were the best. Hey, even Keith D enjoyed that bit.

(By way of context, here's my report from That Night in 2009 (again it was the final Monday), when the flat audience reaction totally threw me. I now recognise a bad night when it happens, and know it's not my fault. Showbiz.)

Thursday, 23 August 2018
Dead Ringer

Another clip from the Scottish Falsetto Socks smashing Edinburgh run of Superheroes - Dead Ringer For Superman. It's on Youtube in subtitled form, or vanilla. Enjoy. There's even a square version on Facebook, if you fancy.

This has been probably the most popular song in the show, with the glasses prop proving a fun if unpredictable bit of slapstick that's different every night. This take is from what I call That Night, the one night when we had an unresponsive audience (as discussed here) and even they laughed at it. Other nights (we

videod three) had better laugh tracks, but not as good prop shots or music mix.

(If you really want to know how it's done, the front-on shot and soundtrack are from Monday Aug 20, and the side shot is from an earlier night).

Thursday, 23 August 2018
Cosmopolitan - new clip from Superheroes

Another new clip from Superheroes, Cosmopolitan. Enjoy. If there was ever an indication that I'm aiming to upload the whole show, it's the fact that I'm uploading a bit of nonsense like this. I'll get onto the meatier scenes next.

Unlike Shakespeare, which had lots of stand-alone sketches which you could watch in isolation, that's really only the case for Superheroes' songs. The comedy routines are all episodes in the plot in this show, which really means

they will mostly only make sense when you watch the full hour.

As I did with Shakespeare, I hope to edit the scenes and upload them piecemeal, then assemble the whole lot together into a concert DVD. The whole hour should go online in the fullness of time. But, like I say, you really have to be there to enjoy the experience.

At time of writing, just 4 shows to go.

Friday, 24 August 2018
"Take a hanky for the tears of laughter you'll cry" - Audience reviews

There's a first for everything. And on Thursday night's show it was The Socks performing minus an eyeball! Just seconds before the show began, I jerked the Sock on the right up and caught it on something, yanking his left eyeball clean off. Luckily it didn't seem to weird too many people out and the show went fine. Audience reviews are, as the Gilded Balloon have been tweeting, the best. And, in our case, they've also proved to be the only reviews we've got (Geek Chocolatenotwithstanding), so we'd best enjoy them. And, delightfully, of the 8 reviews posted by punters on edfringe.com, 7 of them are glowing (the eighth being the one posted by Keith D after "That Night", which we've already discussed). Here they all are.

RTB
Very very good!
Put a huge smile on my face which was still there several days later...kind of like the rictus grin of the Joker... Seriously, well woth going to if you want severely cheered up!

The programme was funny but the improvs were tripply funny! What...a...hoot!

David Robinson
Days at the funniest, sockiest and Scottishest show at the Fringe. It actually hurt to laugh so much. Not only were the scripted bits hilarious, the audience interaction shows that this is a real talent. Why are the socks not on TV? They are far more professional and entertaining than Ant and Dec and much more practical.

Frankie B
Successfully funny. Audience was falling about.
So much better than the big name improv/stand ups we've seen.
Quite clever too behind the apparent simplicity.
This is one show I would actually see again - and I don't think that about many Fringe shows.

Fiona
Loved the socks. This show never fails to make me laugh.

An hour never seems enough. Very talented man and very talented socks. A hilarious hour.

Sue P
Saturday night's brilliant show was a great way to start the week. Might have to see it again! Reccommended.

Frances Mitchell
I admit it, I never really grew up. I like puppet shows and cuddly things, and after finding The Socks on Facebook over a year ago, I've been waiting eagerly for them to come to Edinburgh. I took 3 friends with me, and The Socks didn't disappoint. I can't actually remember the last time I laughed so hard or so long at daft jokes, fun puns and a very clever background of superheroes as diverse as Irn Bru Man and Super Gran. Absolutely hysterical, very clever, and if you're in the mood for some daft, modern, happy fun, then this show should be your shout of choice. (And take a hanky for the tears of laughter you'll cry

Gibletman
'Holey socks, Batman! Is it a bird? Is it a plane?'
'No, old chum, it's the Scottish Falsetto Sock Puppet Theatre...'

Yes, the socks are back and this year they're taking on the subject of superheroes. It was inevitable this topic would eventually get the SFSPT treatment given that puppet master Kev F Sutherland's other job is as a comic-book writer and artist. Oh, and he was once bitten by a radioactive sock which gave him the uncanny ability to speak in a high pitched Scottish accent and hold his hands above his head for extended periods without getting tired...

Unfortunately, Sutherland's familiarity with his subject matter is too big to be contained and the show doesn't entirely translate for a general audience. For instance, why does Spider-Man not appear yet we get the Fantastic Four – an odd decision for a one-man sock puppet theatre where more than two characters on 'stage' at the same time is extremely challenging (although admittedly one of the FF is invisible). There's also an unfathomable 'sub plot' about a long lost racist brother and a song about the Bechdel test that appear to have been rocketed to earth from the exploding remains of an entirely different show.

Nevertheless, the socks' great irresponsibility does lead to some great laughter, and they are still a mainstay of our trips to the Fringe.

To the sockmobile!

Saturday, 25 August 2018
Art at Edinburgh 2018 - a very poor year

Whatever happened to the art at Edinburgh? It's always been the backbone of our visits, the Fringe being complemented by the biggest array of art to be found outside of Venice. Until this year, when we've been met with an endless succession of closed galleries, ex-galleries, galleries that are no longer free, and artwork which is, on the whole, a bit underwhelming.

Top of the list of closed galleries must be the Collective Gallery on Calton Hill, which has frankly been the only reason to climb all the way up Calton Hill for a number of years. It's listed in the Edinburgh Art Festival programme, with a

Summerhall has continued to lose exhibition space to performances over the years. When we first discovered it, it had more art on show than any other venue in years, in all its buildings, and on all its floors. This year there was nothing in the courtyard that now houses a tent theatre, nor in the buildings behind which now house performance spaces and a BBC studio. Even the lower cafe area, which 4 years ago housed one of the most impressive installations, is now just some little used tables. And the exhibition from the DeMarco collection hardly compensates including, as it does, a display of drawings by Orson Welles which have to be the most amateurish display on show this year. A supposed exhibition in the basement was also closed.

whole page to itself, but thank god we found out in advance (from the website) that it's not open.

Add to this the closed basement floor or The City Art Centre, the closed lower level of the National Gallery of Scotland, the broken lift at the National Portrait Gallery (which formerly gave a marvellous all-round view of the exhibition floors), the closed-despite-being-advertised-as-open Burns Monument, no work this year at the High School on Calton Hill, and the closed permanent and the temporary galleries at the National Library of Scotland, and you have quite a diminution of what's been on offer before. You now have to pay to see the exhibitions at Dovecot Gallery, which is a shame, and we didn't bother.

Not that there isn't competition on the "slightly rubbish" front. It would be cruel to single out the Institut Francais's exhibition by Adam Lewis Jacob as the biggest display of "Will This Do" work, but I challenge anyone not to be non-plussed with ennui (how apt the French should have all the bon mots). Similarly disappointing were Tacita Dean at the Fruitmarket (once you've decided she's a bit over-hyped, as I did when she was being a bit dull as a Turner Prize finalist, it's hard to find anything exciting in her work), and the students work at the College Of Art.

So what was good? We enjoyed The Common Sense video piece by Melanie Gilligan and the sound installation by Shilpa Gupta, both at the Art College. Barbara Rae's painting, and the accompanying work at the Royal Scottish Academy was very impressive, outstripping the staid and conservative work one sometimes expects from academicians; Raqib Shaw at the Nat Gall of Modern Art was very interesting, if a bit Roger Dean album cover-y; and Victoria Crowe at the Nat Portrait Gallery was good if you like portraits of famous Scots, and heavy use of the colour brown; Lucy Skaer's curated exhibition at the Talbot Rice was good, but the whole was less than the sum of its parts, and it was made of small and diverse parts.

There were nifty, but slight, installations in a church off the Royal Mile and a bar just behind St Giles, and some lovely films of Edinburgh in the 1950s at Stills

Gallery, but nothing you'd be in a hurry to tell all your friends about.

Most impressive was the Jacobs Ladder exhibition at Ingelby Gallery, in their impressive new location in the New Town. This was complemented by an exhibition at the University Library on George Square, which I've managed to never visit before in my 30 years of coming here. It was good, but not enough on its own to make Edinburgh feel like a town you'd come to to see the art.

And most fun was Rip It Up, the exhibition of artefacts from the history of Scottish pop music. With an excellent TV series to go with it, this was the most memorable exhibition, full of nostalgic

Monday, 27 August 2018
Edinburgh audit 2018

Hev bought me a mug with a Dalek as a Tunnocks teacake. And here we see my Edinburgh haircut, and the new Socks t shirts which, along with the Superheroes comic, sold quite well at the Gilded Balloon shop for the first time.

Another enjoyable Edinburgh comes to an end, with a month having flown by. My show was good, the audiences liked it and so did I, though they didn't come in the numbers I would have liked (see below). Obviously the month was coloured by illness. That of Mum, which saw me leaving town and cancelling shows for the first time; of myself, which saw me getting a cold on day two so having to do shows with next to no voice and drastically reducing my flyering in the first week; and that of Hev, which she doesn't want me to tell you all about, but has caused her a lot of trouble with her diet and, whisper it, included a visit to the Infirmary. We're on top of things now, Mum's in a care home and Hev's slowly figuring out what she can eat, but these things certainly made the month memorable in lots of the wrong ways.

treasures and well produced displays and videos. Not strictly art, but knocking spots off the art for entertainment value.

There is undoubtedly art we haven't seen - we didn't venture out of town, and we weren't going to pay to see the likes of Rembrandt and Canaletto (we may be jaded after the two visits we made to the Venice Biennale last year) - but it wasn't as if we didn't try. Genuinely it would appear that Edinburgh has less art on, in comparison to previous years, and what they have is not as impressive as previous years have had to offer. Other opinions may differ.

We saw lots of art, which was disappointing (as detailed here) and only two shows (as has become the norm, a dreadful state of affairs for which I feel stupidly guilty). I didn't pull a single late night in the Loft Bar and did very little socialising or networking. I flyered, I performed, I sewed sock eyeballs back on and, in fact, made a whole new pair of Socks halfway through the run, I made no videos, and I felt good about my show, while actively planning next year's. The subject will, I think, be the circus and music hall.

More than anything, this month leaves me head-scratching and over-analysing more than I have for many years. Why? Because my sales tanked and I can't work out why.

As recorded in July, my advance sales before the Edinburgh run started were at record-breaking levels and everything was looking good. Then we had the major problem of Mum being not well and me having to leave Edinburgh for two days, coupled with me getting a cold on day two, both of which seriously affected my ability to flyer, and obviously removed two nights from our run. But then, as recorded

in the second week of August, once I returned and got up to speed with flyering, I was finding it wasn't working. And, though the city went from unusually quiet to its normal levels of busy, my flyering continued to be ineffectual.

In 18 years of promoting Edinburgh shows, I have never found flyering to be so unsuccessful. The old "Rule Of Flyering", that one hour's flyering equated to ten bums on seats, is out of the window. I have done five hours of good flyering in one day, and only see half a dozen sales added by the end. As you can see from the graph, whereas every year from 2013 to 2016 ended up with almost exactly the same total sales, this year has ended much lower, just about equalling the Olympic year of 2012. It would have been higher with the

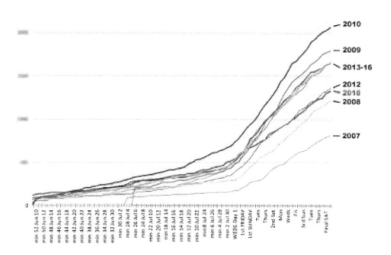

Edinburgh Sales 2018

- 2010
- 2009
- 2013-16
- 2012
- 2018
- 2008
- 2007

two missing days back in there, but not much. What has gone wrong?

To investigate this problem, I've looked at my blogs for the last eight Socks Edinburgh shows, seeing how many days were spent doing Comic Art Masterclasses (and thus unable to flyer), how many reviews I got, and other significant media coverage:

2009 - some reviews inc 4 star Scotsman, lots of classes, on GMTV & BBC Edinburgh - 2nd biggest sales ever
2010 - 6 reviews, Scotsman interview, included in 2 Top Tens, on Culture Show, on One Show, no classes - biggest sales ever
2012 - 11 reviews, 2 shows a day,

Olympic year - after a year off sales plummet from last time
2013 - 9 reviews, 12 days classes & caricatures, Sitcom Trials - sales reach good level
2014 - 3 reviews, 12 days classes, Newsnight & Edinburgh Extra - sales equal last year
2015 - 6 reviews, 8 days classes, noted successful flyering, 3rd week slump - sales equal last year
2016 - 7 reviews, 0 days classes, sales hold up
2018 - 1 review, 4 days classes, flyering ineffectual, after a year off sales holed below the waterline

I have no answer to this question. I take small consolation in hearing the horror stories of other acts, one of whom I spoke to said that, if she got 7 people in on her final night, she'd have been seen by a total of 100 people all month. That puts my moaning in context (I've been seen by over 1300, and am only moaning cos last time I was here that figure was 1600).

Things that used to be a novelty at Edinburgh and have now reached saturation:

Silent Discos
10 foot high posters of comedians
Drag queens with beards
Musicals about Brexit or Trump
Rain

So, as we head home, and struggle to remember The Hot Summer Of 2018 which seems years ago now (it ended the second we arrived in Scotland) I look forward to a busy week of schools, beginning Tuesday. I'll update the notes below when I have a chance to research other peoples' Edinburgh stories. Here's to next year.

Other stories:

Edinburgh Fringe crowds grow by nearly a million in a decade - The Scotsman
(Article includes Fringe up 9% on last year, up 52% on 2009; Space

THIS IS IT IN A NUTSHELL:

COST OF THE SHOW (INC. PROMO & MARKETING): £1,313.40
PLUS LIVING COSTS FOR AUGUST: £772.10
TOTAL COST:£2,085.50

TOTAL MADE IN BUCKET DONATIONS: £1,599.30

sees 11% increase on last year; Official Festival slumped by £500,000 on last year's takings)

Andy Quirk's financial breakdown of his two Free Fringe shows - with graphs!
Reflections of a First Timer by Julian Lee
Underbelly's record breaking 2018 figures
Pleasance's record breaking 2018 figures
Comedy Guide's overview of all the Edinburgh Fringe 2018 stories (a good round-up of things I missed all month)

Comedian Sian Docksey's financial breakdown on her Free Fringe show (from which this is just one slide):
Shappi Khorsandi on the politics of reviewers
Brendon Burns announces he's retiring from Edinburgh
Brett Goldstein's stats (via @brettgoldstein)

Friday, 31 August 2018
Granny's School of Unbelievable Slushies - comics by kids

It's a testament to how all-consuming Edinburgh is, when you're doing the Fringe, that it's taken me until the 2nd of September to get these four comics coloured. But coloured they are, and they're the result of the few Comic Art Masterclasses I did in August while based in Edinburgh. These two are from South Queensferry and Kirkliston libraries. I wisely limited myself to one class in a day, so I wouldn't jeapordise my voice for that night's show, and only lined up 4 days of classes. A far cry from past years, when for example in August 2015 I did at least 8 classes and zoomed off to do classes in Nairn the day after my last show, in August 2014 I produced these and these, and in August 2013 I produced all this lot. What was I thinking? (One thing I wasn't thinking was that I had to colour them all in full colour! When did that madness start?)

These two comics were from libraries in Denny and Meadowbank, both near Falkirk, so an excuse to drive past The Kelpies every time. Not, it has to be said, the most inspiring titles of the year.

This month's libraries got some nice flipcharts, by dint of me turning up in time to do a bit of doodling. Here are two of them.

The celebrities these four groups chose to appear in my demonstration strip were Robert Downey Junior, Johnny Depp, Donald Trump and Beyonce.

Saturday, 1 September 2018
Still Got It - drawings by Mum

Mum's cartoon of the day she was moved from the hospital in Harborough to the Knoll by a taxi driver who seemed to be outstandingly inept. Having asked to be paid in cash, he stopped by the cashpoint and promptly ran out of petrol. Being only half a mile from the Knoll, he then wheeled Mum in a wheelchair up the road, in the rain. Not what she was hoping for. But at least it inspired this drawing, so there's that.

Mum, as you'll know if you've been following this blog, has recently been admitted to a care home. She's in the Knoll in Kibworth, which used to be my mate Nick's house, as her condition continues to be stable but, as she might describe it, boring. She really has

could well be the boss for all I know, I've not met him yet. He's been putting pictures up on the wall for Mum, mostly photos of the family, and her watercolour of "General Jacks" (the Old House in Kibworth Harcourt, which we've always known by that name.)

Here's Jude, Paul, and Mum's zimmer frame. She's not in a hurry to go downstairs and eat with the others, preferring her quiet wee room. I say quiet, Jude (with the tiniest help from me) has sorted out Mum's TV, and iPlayer on her Hudl (Earth's most useless tablet) and iPhone, as well as sorting out a booster for her Wifi. Sadly it's also Earth's slowest wifi, so the only way we can load Mum up with TV is to take the devices home and bring them back loaded. But it seems to be doing the trick.

precious little energy, wanting to sleep most of the time, and is having increasing difficulty with her manual dexterity - a pox on whoever designed phones that you have to tap and swipe in order to answer them, and to all those designers with their nimble fingers who think pinching and swiping with two fingers without accidentally pressing the wrong bit of the screen remains easy forever!

So it's a delight to see her still drawing. Not anything near as much as she's always done, and inevitably not up the quality of her usual work. But I'd happily rank her work alongside late Picassos and a good few others I've seen (this summer's show or Orson Welles drawings at Summerhall springs to mind).

This is a sketch of Paul, who is, I believe, the handyman here at the Knoll. I may be belittling his job, he

I've just been visiting her, over Friday night and through Saturday, my first visit since the first week of August when I came down to help Jude suss out care homes. Jude has been a far better daughter than me, staying with Mum for a few days every week. I'm going to try and get up as often as I can, but the nature of work means it won't be as long as anyone would like.

Sunday, 2 September 2018
Hey Bucket Heads! - comics by kids

No sooner was I back from a month away at the Edinburgh Fringe then I was back at the chalkface doing the last Comic Art Masterclasses of the summer holidays. Of course the kids of Scotland had gone back to school a fortnight ago, hence the end of the Edinburgh classes, but in England they still had another week to go, and this was how they filled it. By flocking to libraries and art centres and enduring classes with me. On Tuesday it was Andover, where they came up with these two cracking titles.

On Wednesday I drove all the way to Sevenoaks and back, which amounted to over 7 hours driving for less than 6 hours work, such is my life. I was pleased with the Bloodsucking Cow cover. By the way, if you're a regular reader of this blog, you've probably worked out that you can see how many kids were in each class by the number of drawings they've done in the backgrounds of the covers. Sevenoaks was a proper sellout, with just short of 30 in each group, as was Andover before it.

In Tewkesbury we had a slightly

smaller turnout, and likewise at Matson library in the afternoon, but both grand groups to work with. And I was chuffed with my Ninja Granny cover. Sometimes a design, knocked off in minutes while the kids are getting on with their drawings, comes off. And just as often it doesn't. Being rested after the month in Edinburgh probably helped.

I say rested. Obviously I was doing a show every night and didn't have time to colour any comics while I was there, but I had a rest from comics drawing. And from driving. Which I certainly got unrested from this week. Monday I drove from Edinburgh to Clevedon, Tuesday to Andover & back, Weds to Sevenoaks in Kent & back, Thursday to Tewkesbury & Matson and then to Warrington for an overnight stay before the day's classes (above), then to Kibworth on Friday night to see Mum, before coming home Saturday night. Enough miles for you?

The celebrities these 8 groups chose to appear in my demonstration strip were Simon Cowell, Donald Trump (twice), The Queen, Harry Hill (twice), Ant McPartlin and Barack Obama.

Monday, 3 September 2018
Motion Capture

A fun clip from Superheroes, as seen at Edinburgh this year, and soon to go on tour, the Motion Capture routine. Not big, not clever, great fun. Enjoy.

Wednesday, 5 September 2018
Batman v Joker

Another routine from the Socks' Superheroes show, Batman v Joker now online. .

A lovely little audience pleaser, this works well in the context of the show, where the scenes lead into each other, but possibly ends a little suddenly out of context.

Wednesday, 5 September 2018
Avengers Infinity Reel

Another new clip from the Socks' Superheroes show, the Avengers routine followed by the Avengers Inifinity Reel. Another couple of corking bits from the show, the first part of which you might recognise from its appearance in 2013's Socks In Space. Waste not a good bit, say I.

Friday, 21 September 2018
Writing Joseph

I've written another story for Bible Society, this time Joseph. Following on from the Women Of The Bible, which I now have sample copies of that I'm taking into schools, along with feedback forms (hopefully we'll see it published soon), this is my latest commission and it's been great fun to write.

Notable has been the conditions under which I've produced it. It was done entirely while sat in a fold-up chair in the back room of Heather's recent exhibition. Whereas I'd normally sprawl over the desk in my office, paper strewn everywhere, and my laptop waiting for the second stage of the writing, this time it was all done with no space to play with and, literally, on my lap.

Stage one is scribbling the story out in biro. That's where the gags come, the visuals get dreamt up, and the first bit of editing happens. That took two days in the gallery (which we set up on Monday and took down the following Sunday).

Step two of my Bible stories is writing all the words into the voice bubbles, which will then be the bubbles of the finished printed artwork. This method is how Harvey Kurtzman and Bill Gaines used to do EC comics 65 years ago. They'd type all the text onto the artboard and supply that to the artist to draw on top of. Well, it's my method too. That stage took two days too.

Step three, usually, is for me to draw rough visual versions of every panel, and it is this that get

supplied to the editor to approve. And that's where I stalled this time round. As you can see from the sample above, drawing straight onto the computer screen via the graphics tablet, sat on my lap, is not something at which I excel. I need to do that bit at a drawing board in my studio, and can take another two days. So I decided against it, and instead sent me editor Rachel a script that looked like this.

Luckily for me, not only could she understand the story from text alone, but also she liked it. So the script was delivered to her Friday afternoon and, following a phone call on Thursday morning, I had a couple of pages of rewrites to do and we have a 23 page story ready for me to draw.

The rewrites, to keep up the novelty working method, were done while sat by Mum's bed in The Knoll care home in Kibworth. I was there all day Thursday, stopping off en route from two days at schools in North Lincs. Two pages of new material, scribbled, laid out and delivered from another fold up chair.

I'll be doing the artwork in my office. And, spoiler alert, it will be the last piece I do there before I have to move out of my office.

It's good to write and draw comics for a living, I'd love to do more of it. I look forward to delivering a story I'm happy with. Stay tuned.

Friday, 14 September 2018
Hev's Lulu Exhibition

This week has been spent invigilating Hev's latest exhibition, at the Christmas Steps Gallery in Bristol, and a lovely looking thing it is. Half of it is a selection of Anubis work, including a photo series taken last year at the Venice Biennale, and the other half is her new work in progress on the subject of Lulu. Lulu is the subject of one of her recent articles and a book that's underway, and the exhibition includes a new sculpture based on Lulu, and a set of canvasses based on the photos that have come from Hev's research.

How's this for a work in progress from the work in progress? These images of Lulu, and the enigmatic

El Nino, are printed on actual pages from Times newspapers from 1889. Sweet.

The Private View was an absolute triumph, with a marvellous turnout of people, bringing together friends in a great party atmosphere, along with Heather's new contacts from Circus 250 and the gallery world. All in all a great success. And I even got my RCA Secret postcards drawn while we were there:

Saturday, 22 September 2018
Leaving the office

So it came to pass that in the first week of September, Gerry my landlord rang me up and told me the time had come to move out of my office.

I'm surprised it hasn't happened earlier, to be honest. I've been luxuriating in a large office space, which has filled up more and more with my junk until it is 90% storage unit and 10% work space, since I moved in sixteen - yes sixteen - years ago. My first action? To put some stuff on eBay. Above you see one of the two Socks massive posters, which went as a pair for £75 the lot.

One thing that's not shifting fast on eBay is my cheese plant - if anyone wants it it's going cheap. It's eight feet high, reaching from floor to ceiling and filling the window. Wherever I move to next, I fear Cheesey (no, she/they've never had a name, I just call the leaves Them) won't fit.

Most likely I'm going to be spending a while trying to work from home, while the contents go into storage. It won't be the first time.

Looking back at where I've managed to work over the years is an interesting bit of nostalgia:

1989 - When we moved to the South West, and I went freelance for the first time, I began my solo career drawing comic strips in the back bedroom of 5 The Glebe in Wrington. Writing and drawing

between a portable drawing board and an Amstrad green-screen "everybody's first word processor". Here I produced the rest of my strips for Gas and The Damage, then edited, wrote and drew for UT comic (91 - 93) as well as producing a daily strip, Battler Britten, for the Daily Sport, and a weekly football strip for the Sunday Sport. I was busy, if not necessarily doing work I was proudest of.

strips for Gas, The Damage, and Century 21's poster magazines, I managed it all on one table. My Amstrad computer would be moved on, and my drawing board moved off the table top in turn. The centrepiece of my organisation was the fax machine. Try explaining one of those to the kids today. Out of the window I watched the great storm of spring 1990, including a chimney pot flying through the window of a greenhouse. I was there for 6 months.

1990 - 93 - While Heather worked at Nailsea school every day, I worked from the back room of our flat in Leagrove Road. That back room still doubled as a guest bedroom at the time, and I shared my workspace with the fold up Z-Bed that had come from Kibworth. Again it was a tabletop shared

93 - 95 - My first office, on Old Street in Clevedon. With the creation of Gladiator comic, which I devised and brought to a publisher, negotiating the licensing deal with LWT and looking forward to a smash hit, I took on the role of writer and artist, and realised I could possibly expand my organisation. So I rented an office, and brought Lucy Allen in as an assistant. Then Mark Buckingham asked if he could come and share my office, and I welcomed him with open arms. Thanks to Mark I was able to break into Marvel comics. When Gladiators went tits up, losing me money and threatening an end to my work in comics, I helped Mark out with some inking, and gradually crept up to doing my own inking for Marvel on Dr Strange and Star Trek. In this office I also designed t-shirts for Network,

including Xmas 93's best seller "Let's Get Out There And Twat It"

95 - 98 - Our second office. At the suggestion of Steve Noble, Mark and I moved to a bigger suite of offices above the then Midlands Bank on Sixways. Don't look for it, it's not there any more. Here I inked Marvel comics as Mark made the wise move to drawing for DC, and was also beginning my fledgling stand up career. It was in this office that Situations Vacant, the live sitcom shows that were to become The Sitcom Trials, was born. Our first meeting, which included Iain Morris long before he created The Inbetweeners, took place in Steve & Rob's board room. Meanwhile, as the Marvel comics work started to dry up (the company filed for Chapter 11 bankruptcy, the details of which you'll find on Wikipedia) Mark and I launched The National Comics Awards from this office, and I began plans for Comics 99.

98 - 2002 - Back home. With my Marvel work gone, I struggled to find comics work, and was even reduced to training to sell double glazing. I was unable to afford my share of the office rent, so Mark and I both had to move out of our beautiful loft suite. Three rooms we had! Three rooms! It's since been converted into a flat which, with an extension out across the roof, is worth about £400,000. Meanwhile most of my stuff, which was an awful lot of comics and old artwork, went into storage, firstly at Hugh's picture framing company behind the garage by Salthouse Fields, and later in a barn on a farm near Weston Super Mare. I moved back to working from the back room. Something that was about to become a lot more difficult when Heather left her job at Nailsea school.

Summer/Autumn 2002 - The farm. I rented an office in a spider-lined damp subterranean stone room on a farm, a mile down the road to Nailsea. There couldn't have been a worse place for me to work and I hated it. I came back to working there having finished my loss-making second year at the Edinburgh Fringe, with the second Sitcom Trials show and my only solo stand up show, and I was both impoverished and miserable. But luckily I'd come back with the promise of a TV show. First I had the 8 week Rude Health TV show, and then coming in spring 2003 there was to be the Sitcom Trials TV show. It looked like I was about to have some money again, and another office loomed on the horizon.

(A shot from 2014, compare the size of the cheese plant then and now, above)

2002 - 2018 - The Office. Thanks to Gail Buckingham (Mark's then wife) I was introduced to Gerry and the office on Copse Road, which had been Mark's office ten years earlier, before the two of us moved into Old Street. The cork notice board on my wall was made my Mark's dad. I moved in in September or October 2002 and have remained there ever since. It's in this room that I've written and drawn all of my comic strips for The Beano, and my Women Of The Bible graphic novel, and a hundred other script and art commissions. Notes from the Sitcom Trials TV show are still on my walls, along with the certificates I got from Childline and Comic Relief for the

money I raised from my comic festivals, which had started being run from home, and ended in 2004.

The most visible items on the wall are of course the posters for the Scottish Falsetto Sock Puppet Theatre. Every studio video they've made has been shot here. Their green screen has hung permanently on the wall, and their props and the components for making props, take up a big table in the middle of the room. There are also currently a few boxes of their comics and t shirts taking up a bit of space. Though not nearly as much space as Heather's Anubis sculptures, who have lived here characterising the room from the start.

(This photo from 2014 shows the place less cluttered than it is now)

So, not-quite-everything must go. Looking around I see an awful lot of Doctor Who toys that ought to find a better home (how many

Tardisses?), and quite a bit of computer hardware. The Amstrad has long gone, but there's still space being taken up by a black Mac Power PC, a round-backed 2002 iMac, a large-screened 2005 iMac, two toilet-seat MacBooks (circa 2001/2), and a white MacBook that I was still working on up till 2013. What do you do with old Macs?

Can I really work from home? Or will there be office space that I can realistically afford? With my work in schools, and touring with the Socks in recent years, there have been months when I don't use the office at all. Since 2007, it's been deserted throughout August for all but two year, for example, and spending more than 100 days doing classes, it spends a lot of its time lying dormant. One thing I won't be needing any more is a phone line, with the mobile now taking all calls, and the broadband having long since replaced the fax machine (it went to the tip, that's what you do with those).

Let us see what the next six weeks hold. I have take a Big Yellow Self Storage unit, and I've got a really heavy workload to take me all the way through October. November will find me in a new working space, who knows where?

Tuesday, 25 September 2018
Cobsick Planet Of Poo Poo - comics by kids

These comics are the fruits of two days in a row at St Barnabas school, and its neighbour Kirmington, in North Lincolnshire. I stayed over in Brigg, which is a pretty little place. I'm particularly happy with the cover for Cobsick Planet Of Poo Poo, which is not only a great title, but which coloured up nicely.

I do all this colouring in spare moments in the evening after each class and, honestly, waste a little more time on them than is truly justified. It's not like we're ever going to make a best selling coffee table book out of these babies. But once you've started something like this, it's hard to stop. I hope the kids appreciate the after-care they're getting for free there.

Furze Down school in Bucks is for kids with special educational needs, making it all the more delightful when they achieve the final results which they did here. Their comic strips are tucked away inside, a taste of which you can see in the doodles they add to the covers. The titles are all theirs.

The celebrities these six group chose to star in the demonstration strip that I draw on the flipchart were Donald Trump, Robbie Williams, Kim Kardashian, Simon Cowell (twice), and David Walliams.

Sunday, 7 October 2018
Socks Go To Denmark

Well that's easy for you to say. Let's just hope everyone understands our Scottish accents as, starting tomorrow, we return to Denmark.

To be honest I can't remember whether we've been twice or three times before. Certainly I blogged a

little about our visit to Aarhus in 2011, and it looks like the last time we went was October 2012 when the Socks took a version of Boo Lingerie to Aarhus and Copenhagen, sharing the bill with Andrew Vincent. That was when we shot a version of The Killing sketch, which went down great over there.

So now we're making our return, with a rather mind-blowing ten dates lined up. And the oddest thing about these dates is that, for 5 of them, our brief is to do a show about Brexit. At time of writing, ie the day before the first gig, I've written a show but not performed it yet, which includes new material they'll be seeing for the first time, threaded through the best of our Shakespeare show. It won't be until the first night that we'll be able to

assess what works and what doesn't. So it's back to where we were in February when we first tested out Superheroes in Leicester.

The schedule looks like this:

8. Oct. Silkeborg, Campus Bindenslevs plads - Brexit show
9. Oct. Harders, Svendborg - Brexit show
10. Oct. Ebbeltoft, Det Gamle Posthus - Brexit show
11 - 14 Oct Katapult, Aarhus - Superheroes show
15. Oct. Kjellerup, Den Gamle Biograf - Brexit show
16. Oct. Uldum, Uldum Højskole kl - Brexit show

The Superheroes show, which we're doing for 5 nights at our familiar venue of Katapult, gives us the first chance to do the

The Scottish Falsetto Sock Puppet Theatre (UK)

9/10
Gratis Entré
Dørene Åbner kl. 19.00
Show starter kl. 20.00

THE SCOTTISH FALSETTO SOCK PUPPET THEATRE er en af de britiske aers mest omtalt Teater acts det sidste årti. Med Breatt Socks and superheroes kommer de med deres humoristiske og refleksionsskabende bud på hvordan Breatt, ser ud for dem og den enkelte englændere, samt hvad det kommer til at få at kernsreivenøer og hvordan forholdet bliver til resten af EU.

Pressen skrev:

Had every single audience member... laughing until they cried." ★★★★★
Edinburgh Evening News

Edinburgh material since Edinburgh. And, to my surprise, re-reading the script I've found it to be even funnier than I'd remembered. As for the gags which won't mean anything to a Danish audience, that'll be what we discover from the 11th. I remember one of the biggest surprise doing Boo Lingerie in Aarhus in 2012 was the discovery that Charles Dickens is totally unfamiliar to Danish audiences. Let's see what they make of the references to Diddy David Hamilton, Hamilton Academicals, and Acker Bilk. Probably less than the audiences in Edinburgh did (and plenty of them didn't understand that bit... you know, I think I'm going to be replacing that bit, aren't I?)

Thursday, 11 October 2018
Kev on The Apprentice

Of course I missed it cos I'm in Denmark, but if you want to see my brief appearance on The Apprentice last night, it's to be found here on iPlayer. (I can't make it work while I'm over here, and am wary of downloading dodgy VPN software while I'm here, just in case, so I'll see it when I get home next week). By all accounts I didn't disgrace myself. Thanks to Hev for the screengrab above.

"Awesome side eye from Kev Sutherland on The Apprentice there...   " - Sarah Niblock via Facebook""

Thanks to John Freeman for the graphic above. Since he and Hev both grabbed the self same moment, I can guess my appearance was very much a cough and a spit. We recorded it back in May at the Beano Studios offices in London, with myself and Nigel Auchterlounie drawing the two comic strips, his for the girls team, mine for the boys. I have no idea how much made it onto screen. I leaked a tiny snippet in my blog at the time (when I was still keeping schtum). Here's more of the Benji Saves The Day, as snapped on the day.

Looking at the art again, I far prefer my scribbles, drawn while they were talking, to the finished line art which I did on the wrong type of paper with the wrong pen (all my bad choices) so it looked very weak. I'm betting Nigel's was a much stronger line drawing.

UPDATE: I found the whole episode on Youtube, put up rather randomly by someone within a day of broadcast. My bit is indeed a cough and a spit, and the tiniest glimpse we get of the pages shows that they look fine. The respective quality of Nigel's and my art also had no bearing whatsoever on the result of the task. Here's the little I managed to snap:

The comments online have been nice, here's a taste.

John Freeman's Down The Tubes review

Jamie Smart @jamiesmart .@KevFComicArtist and @spleenal on #Theapprentice2018! Bloody heroes

Ric Lumb @PuttyCAD The only super heroes in this episode of #TheApprentice
Whytrig MiddleSchool @WhytrigMS Think we might have spotted @KevFComicArtist on @bbcapprentice tonight. We recognised the braces!
Vince @VinceStadon Once a year I turn on my telly, and there, unexpectedly, is @KevFComicArtist. feel haunted.
PJ Holden @ COMIC CITY! Verified account @pauljholden It's @KevFComicArtist because of course it is! #theapprentice ▪▪▪
✎ @InspiredMind5 Thought I recognised those braces! Congrats - great to see
Jason Manly No wonder you have

Friday, 12 October 2018
Facebook trivia roundup

fled the country Kev Sutherland

Ben Morton @MidBoulevard Hear
hear! Fantastic work all around
You all smashed it regardless!
ComicScene UK Magazine
@comicsflixukus Should have had
the sock puppets saying what it
looks like you are really thinking!
That would be great TV! Bog Eyed
Books
@BogEyedBooks Great to see
@phoenixcomicuk and
@BeanoOfficial on
#Theapprentice2018! Well done
@KevFComicArtist, your face said
it all! #KidsLoveComics
 Nigel Auchterlounie   @spleenal
IN YOUR FACE
@KevFComicArtist !!!

During a busy month of drawing
comics, clearing out the office, then
gigging for ten days in Denmark,
I've still found time to write trivial
nonsense on Facebook. Here's
some of it.

Got to move out of the office, so
putting my worldly (workly) goods
in storage. Made a start yesterday.
But blimey norah you build up quite
the mountain of crap when you've
been around this long, with a
tendency to keep everything.
Every time I pack a box I'm going
through the whole "Do I need this?
Will I ever read this again? Should I
put it on eBay? Who has time for
that, I'll put it in a box again"
process. Yesterday, for example, I
boxed up 15 years worth of Q
magazines (starting with issue 8 if
you're interested. And no, they're
going in storage cos they won the
"It'll be worth something someday"

debate.) Anyone else thrown out 30 years worth of shit / stroke / put it all in storage, recently?

I'm puzzled about this Joe Sugg chap (off of Strictly). It says on Wikipedia that he's the author of a graphic novel. It then says "the writing is by Matt Whyman, with artist Amrit Birdi". So which bit is he the author of? I, as far as most kids I teach are concerned, am the author of The Beano, by the way.

There's a film on Talking Pictures TV called The Scamp, with a young Australian boy in the lead. Whatever happened to him, you wonder? The answer is brilliant... http://www.brothersgibb.org/reports-colin-petersen.html

Bloody hell Baldrick! I've just found the worst feature of the new iPlayer design yet. When you've finished listening to one show, it plays you the start of a totally different one, from a station you never listen to! I went from an episode of Counterpoint to the Radio 1 Breakfast Show, and now I've gone from an excellent documentary on 4 Extra to the morning show on Radio Leicester! Madness. (The above grab was from another occasion when it gave me a Welsh language show! It's also given me a Gaelic show. Madness.)

Jaws When did you last watch Jaws? It's on Netflix and we watched it last night. Wow. It's a lesson in film making, and I can't imagine what it must have been like seeing it in 1975 when there hadn't been a film anything like it since Hitchcock more than a decade earlier. Exemplary. You get touches of Hitchcock (eg the contra-zoom), bits of Mike Nichols (the realistic dialogue in deep-focus

shots), and a few bits of Buster Keaton (the comic timing where you think you're safe, then you think you're in danger, then you're not, then you are). Then you get bits that are pure Spielberg (the end of the pier turns round in the water and starts chasing you and so many more). If he didn't invent the techniques he uses, and he often did, Spielberg brought them back into use after years of neglect, and with Jaws set the mould for the modern action film that is still our expectation today. Everything from Pirates of the Caribbean to The Lego Movie can trace its stylistic origins to this movie.

It's not Wagon Wheels that got smaller, it was the NME. It's only while chucking them out of my office I've realised the NME kept shrinking by an inch every couple of years right up until I, and everyone else, stopped getting it. Probably cos it was hidden behind some Wagon Wheels. (The

photo's not clear, but the 1998 copies are 40cm tall, the 2008 ones are 30cm.)

 In response to Vince's post asking for bands named after insects I wrote:
I am so pleased with my pathetic contribution to this thread, I couldn't resist sharing it. So, how many bands named after insects can you think of?
I got (with a bit of Googling, admittedly):
The Roaches
The Cockroaches
Moth
Bugs
Caterpillar
Centipedes
The Termites
Earwig
Silverfish
Scarab
Larva
Silkworm
WASP
B Bumble & The Stingers
The Butterfly Effect
Bee Band
Tse Tse Fly
WORM
Flat Worms
Insect Warfare
White Moth Black Butterfly

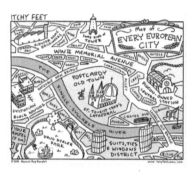

ITCHY FEET

Friday, 12 October 2018
Drawing in my hotel room

Alien Ant Farm
and Papa Roach
Your turn.

I'm currently in Aarhus in Denmark, and from my window can see Some Kind Of Tower. Last night I performed in the Cobblestone Alley area, tonight I think I'm near Crates & Cranes. Earlier this year I was in Hannover which has the most Postcardy Old Town, made up from the few non-bombed pre-war buildings, which have all been moved from where they used to be, to create a square that looks like a quasi old town. At least here in Denmark they had the good sense to just be collaborators and so not get bombed to buggery by the Brits.

Happiness is managing to get proper comic strip drawing done on the table in your hotel room
#comics #myactualjob

Thanks to the marvels of bluetooth and cloud technology, I'm getting a lot of these random photos turning up on my laptop, with me in daft poses pulling stupid faces. Why could this be, you ask? It's because they've transferred to my computer from my phone before I've been able to erase them. And why have I taken them in the first place? Because Joseph.

If you look closely you'll see the hands from the above photo were what I used as reference for the first picture on this page of Joseph, the 23 page graphic novel I've written and am drawing for Bible Society. My deadline of the end of October looms ever close, meaning every spare moment in my hotel room has to be spent drawing. I also have, on my to do list, a drawing for the sleeve of a podcast

CD and a rather elaborate Christmas card with 87 different drawings on it! Bloody hell Baldrick!

Working hunched over the little glass table in my hotel room is not, I'm sure, doing my spine any good. In fact I can feel some twinges and look forward to getting back to my drawing board next week, but at least this hotel has a table, and indeed very good light. So onwards and upwards.

Here, purely for my benefit, is a log of what I've drawn so far:

Script written during Hev's exhibition and sent to Rachel, my editor, Fri Sept 14.
Script amends delivered Sept 20
By Weds Sept 26 Pages 1 - 3 pencilled & inked, p4 pencilled
Sept 26 - Fri Oct 5 Pages 4 - 10 pencilled & inked before Denmark (with a few days off to put boxes in storage).

Oct 9 - 12 (in Denmark) Pages 11 - 15 pencilled
Quarter past midnight Oct 12th, Page 15 inked, 11 - 15 borders & bubbles inked, & one panel on each page inked. After a very good Socks Superheroes gig in Aarhus, might I add.

UPDATE: Sat Oct 13, 4 pages inked before lunchtime.
Page 16 pencilled between lunchtime and 5pm show, and inked by 9.20pm. Approx 4 hrs total.
Sun Oct 14, page 17 pencilled by 10.30am, then off to see Aros art gallery.
2pm - 3.15, page 18 pencilled.
7pm - 9.30, page 19 pencilled (I'm a lot slower in the evenings)
Mon Oct 15, page 20 pencilled by midday. Page 21 pencilled by 12.50 - fastest page yet!

Allowing for a trip to Manchester and Bodelwyddan next weekend, and three days gigging on the 25th - 27th, I have 6 more drawing days left in October when I get home. And that's if I delay moving out of my office. Oh yes, and all 23 pages need colouring. God, the agony of being busy with comic art for once in my life!

2pm - 3.30, page 22 pencilled. Only one page left!

4.45 - Yes! Page 23, the final page, pencilled! Just in time for me to go off to tonight's Socks gig at 5pm. Tues Oct 16, 3 pages inked between 9am and 4.15pm. So each page takes 2.33333 recurring hours to ink.

4.15 - 4.55/ 10.30 - 11.15pm a fourth page inked, finishing after the final Denmark Socks gig. Weds Oct 17, 10am one more page inked, have to check out in an hour, so that'll be my lot

WOW! 11am - checked out having got another page inked!!

Oh yes, and I do have to prepare and perform a comedy show every night here in Denmark, which in the case of the first three gigs has involved up to 4 hours travelling each day. Sigh. I tell you one thing I don't have time for, fannying about writing this bloody blog!

So my final Denmark work rate was...

Oct 9 - 12 - 5 pages pencilled

Oct 13 - 1 page pencilled, 5 pages inked

Oct 14 - 3 pages pencilled

Oct 15 - 4 pages pencilled

Oct 16 - 4 pages inked (3 still to ink)

Oct 17 - 2 pages inked (only 1 to go)

Tuesday, 16 October 2018
Socks tour of Denmark

Thanks to Tommy Neilsen for this shot of the Socks in concert in Kjellerup on the penultimate night of our 9 night tour. Yes, I thought the light was a bit purpley. Regardless, it was the best night yet.

And thanks indeed to Tommy for organising this whole tour. I don't think anyone's organised such a successful tour run for us before. Nine consecutive nights, five nights in different small towns giving them our specially written Brexit show, and four nights in Aarhus giving them our Superheroes show. And every night has been excellent (at time of writing we still have to play Uldum, so there's still scope for it going tits up at the end, but fingers crossed).

The Brexit shows have EU funding because of their partly educational component, and as a result are all done for a flat fee, plus my travel and accommodation is covered. The four Superheroes shows are being done for a small guarantee and a door split which, having had one sellout, and two shows at 75% full (in a 50 seater, the smallest crowd being fifteen), we'll have done alright on those too.

The Brexit shows - in the library in Silkeborg, a pub theatre in Svendborg, a community arts centre in Ebeltoft, a converted cinema in Kjellerup and (to come) a high school in Uldum - have been free to the public, so we had no idea how many would be there until it kicked off. Surprisingly, for 8pm on a weekday night, we've had great turnouts of around 30 per show, with our final night having a guaranteed sitting-duck crowd of maybe 100. Tommy has introduced us each time - entirely in Danish, so I've no idea what he said and,

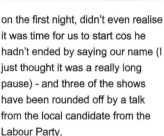

on the first night, didn't even realise it was time for us to start cos he hadn't ended by saying our name (I just thought it was a really long pause) - and three of the shows have been rounded off by a talk from the local candidate from the Labour Party.

So what have I given them, in my brand new hour long specially-written Brexit show? Well, before you start thinking I can turn out a brand new hour of comedy gold on any theme at short notice, I'm sorry to disappoint, but the show actually comprises a lot of stuff from other shows, wrapped around the new themed stuff. The running order is:

Intro gags and I'm A Sock song
The Killing - done in Denmark in 2012
Doublets & Ruffs - from 2016's Shakespeare (with Danish additions, eg CBBC has become Ramashang. This & Forbrydelsen are the only Danish references which get a laugh)
Brexit Word Association - NEW
Travel gags - from 2010's On The Telly
Walk On Wild Side - from 2008's Return
Magic - from Telly
UKIP Song - from 2014's And So Am I
Nigel Farage routine - NEW
An Actor Prepares - from Shakespeare
Insults - from Shakespeare
F Up Some Shakespeare - from Shakespeare
Farage on Immigration - NEW
Stereotypes - from And So Am I
Eurovision Routine - NEW
Gary Barlow Eurovision Song - NEW (done on Youtube 2017)

Farage persuades public - NEW
Richard III (first part) - from
Shakespeare
Break up & All By Myself song -
from Return, as redone for 2018's
Superheroes
Theresa May - NEW
Sweary Poppins - from Return

So there you have it. A show with
routines which help tell the story,
but are also tried and tested, and
with a lot of incidental Shakespeare
in. But, as you'll know if you've
seen those routines, the point of
them is not their Shakespearian
content but the conflict between the
two Socks, so they worked very
well. The audiences have loved it.
The whole show got a rewrite after
the first night, inevitably, with the
order changing, and some new
material coming in. But after night
two we stuck with the same

structure, and the adlibs built
around the lines, as they always do
as a show beds in.

After three nights of Brexit, we then
had a four night run at Teater
Katapult in Aarhus, giving them our
hour long Superheroes show, as
performed at Edinburgh. In fact we
gave them a 75 minute show,
because that's what it said in the
programme (something I'd clearly
agreed to on the phone, not a
problem). The simple insertion of
Michael Jackson's Earth Song in
the middle, and the addition of
Sweary Poppins at the end, and
suddenly the show is 75 minutes
long.

To begin with I didn't remove or
translate any gags, deciding to run
them past the Danish audience and
get humour from what worked and

what didn't. Jokes that had to go or change included:

Bob Kane - Bobbing up and down doesn't mean anything in Danish Motion Capture - Jobby had to be translated to Hoondepude, which then got the laugh every time
Dinner dinner dinner dinner Batman - This reference didn't mean anything because, although they'd seen the 1960s Batman series, they don't call dinner dinner. Got laughs discovering and commenting on this.
Degrasse Tyson - The kneel / Neil pun didn't register
Scottish Superheroes - For the record Oor Wullie is even less well known in Denmark than in England, and Guardians Of The Deep Fried Galaxy Bar was two cultural references too far
Irn Bru Man - Irn Bru took a lot of explaining, which was luckily fun
Thanos - We had to keep in a pun about Thanos sounding like "Tha knows" in a Yorkshire accent. This also took a lot of explanation, giving us an excuse to go on about Danish pronunciation, which went very well.
Harley and Ivy - manure became fertiliser, DEFRA had to go
… and the rest of the show worked well, with me realising just how

many good visual gags we had, and how universal Marvel & DC superheroes are. The Brother came across well purely as a visual and a relationship, with his Cockney Rhyming Slang, which was lost on everyone, working on its rhythm more than its actual content.

The Superheroes show got better every night, ending on a high with Sunday's show. We also sold 5 copies of the Superheroes comic (having only brought 10, that was not bad).

I've also managed to make great use of my daytime by pencilling and inking the 23 page Joseph strip I'm doing for Bible Society. You can see a record of my progress in this blog here. So all in all a jam packed, and slightly knackering, ten days away from home.

If anyone wants to book the Socks for international dates, we've got the skills to fit the bill. We're getting good at tweaking our wordplay to appeal to foreigners with English as a second language. And if anyone wants a themed show, we seem to do quite well in cherry-picking from our ten previous shows and

it regularly to feel that I'm as good as I could be. I feel awkward about my artwork. I like my humorous style, and I know I'll never be the draughtsmen that I grew up admiring. But it's the colouring about which I am most concerned.

Back in the day, when I was doing colour pages every month for The Damage and others, I used to use water colour and magic markers and started to feel I knew what I was doing. I even painted pages in goache, god help me. Took ages. Since I've had access to Photoshop, which I think came with the Mac I acquired in 1998 (so, another anniversary) I've been entirely self taught, and never sure that I'm doing things as well as I could. So I put a shout out on Facebook to see if anyone had top tips. A few came in.

One thing I was obsessing about was Flatting, which all the colourists of US comics seem to do. So I did it for the example you see on this page. Does it make things quicker? I'm not sure. I've ended up working with a mixture of my previous method, and a couple of techniques like flatting, consistent use of a purple shadow layer, and this time I've decided against selecting and colouring outlines, which I spent a lot of time on in previous strips. Let's see how we get on shall we? Meantime, here are some of the tips that came in on Facebook.

Nigel Auchterlounie First have b&w line art on top layer set to multiply locked. A copy of that under to colour. Fill an empty layer with a base colour inbetween. Set that to multiply and merge with the

sticking it all together to a coherent end.

Thanks again Tommy, this has been fun. Come on Uldum, let's go out with a bang.

PS: Update, Uldum went well too.

Tuesday, 23 October 2018
Colouring Joseph

Having pencilled and inked my 23 page Joseph story for Bible Society (I referred to it as a 23 page graphic novel on Facebook, at which Gordon Rennie pointed out that that's what we call a comic) now I have the task of colouring it all.

It's a strange thing that, after thirty years working as a professional comic artist - and we must have passed that anniversary at some point recently as I had my first work in Oink in 1987 then had my first work accepted by Gas magazine in 1988 and went full time freelance in the summer of 1989 - I still lack confidence in certain areas. The writing I feel most confident about, but even then I don't do enough of

WHAT COULD THAT ALL MEAN?

DO YOU WANT THE *FREUDIAN* INTERPRETATION? OR *SHALL* WE GO WITH *MINE*?

bottom line art copy. This should give you 2 layers. Line art and a copy under that's coloured with one colour. This means anything you miss will still have a colour. Fill gutters and eyes and teeth white. Then all skin tones. Colour things that have to be a particular colour first. Then you're not colouring a jumper green then realising you have to change it because they're standing in front of a green bush. That's all I got. Good luck.

Andrew Dodd The line work I right click the magic wand and select the black in the line art first, creating a black layer that uses the line art as a mask, this can help later when changing the colour of the lines. I block all the colours in and on a separate layer add a hue and saturation layer as a mask for the shadows. This means that if I

change any of the colours, the shadow changes with it. Background on it's own colour, characters on their's.

Gordon Rennie "...a 23 page graphic novel..."
Don't we just call them 'comics'?

Jamie Smart I don't do all that flatting stuff I've never understood it. I do similar to Nigel's method, I'll put 4 b+w pages all on one page and go through dropping one colour in, then repeat with a different colour, etc etc. My Wacom's super helpful to with its shortcut buttons, so my left hand is clicking between wand and painter while my right hand is picking the colours. Good luck with it all!

Chris Okse Oxenbury I discovered this Kev , https://www.ayalpinkus.nl/Flatton.html It creates flats and that .

Kev Sutherland Thanks to Okse for directing me to Flatton. Not sure how useful it'll be, until I can give it a colour guide. Here's my first use of it...

Kev Sutherland But you know, at a push I could live with this for a random panel where colour matching didn't matter(same panel after two minutes tweaking)

UPDATE: Sunday 21st Oct, page **10** coloured
Mon Oct 22 - pages **2 - 4** coloured
Tues Oct 23 - pages **1, 5 - 6** coloured
Weds Oct 24 - pages **7 - 9** coloured
Thurs Oct 25 - Page **11** coloured, then off to Socks gig in Canterbury
Sat Oct 27 - page **21** coloured
Sun Oct 28 - page **22** coloured
Mon Oct 29 - 11.45am p **23** coloured. 1.57pm p **20** coloured. 4.58pm p **12** coloured.
Tues Oct 30 - 7.50am p**13**. 10.27am p**14**. 12.15 p**15**. 3.15pm p**16**. 5.15pm p**17**. 9pm p**18**. Six pages in a day, only one to go!
Weds Oct 31 - page 19, final page, coloured and whole comic delivered & invoiced 11am. Hoorah!

Wednesday, 31 October 2018
Story of Joseph - working diary

At long last, at 11am Oct 31st, I completed and delivered the 23 pages of full colour lettered art that comprised The Story Of Joseph for Bible Society. I'm told some people deliver a job like this every month. All I can say is I'd seriously need to streamline my working methods to manage that on a regular basis.

I have loved drawing this project, as I have my previous strips for Bible Society, and look forward to seeing them in print. But making this workload fit around the rest of my schedule is quite a shenanigans. As it is I have two other art jobs - a Christmas card for Laurence and a CD cover for the SofT podcast, both of which should also be finished by today's deadline and both of which have a way to go yet. So why is this all taking me so long? Three reasons primarily, Socks, schools, and the office, out of which I was supposed to move today.

Gerry, my landlord, gave me two months notice when I'd returned from Edinburgh, on the 1st of September, so I should have been out by now. But look at my

THEN I HAD A **SECOND** DREAM. THERE ARE SEVEN FULL, RIPE **EARS** OF **CORN**, GROWING ON A **SINGLE** STALK

THEN **UP** SPRING SEVEN **THIN** EARS OF CORN, ALL **BLASTED** AND **ROTTEN**. THEN THE **THIN** EARS **SWALLOW** UP THE **RIPE** EARS, AND **STILL** THEY LOOK **THIN**.

AND **HOW** DID THIS MAKE YOU **FEEL**?

HUNGRY, TO BE HONEST

calendar since then.

Sept 10 - 16th was Heather's exhibition. During this time, as co-invigilator, I wrote the script for Joseph.

I've done days at schools in North Lincs (2 days), Avonmouth, Furze Down, Sutton Coldfield, & Manchester.

Oct 8 - 17th I was in Denmark with the Socks, where I pencilled and inked most of Joseph.

Socks gigs have also taken me to Swindon, Lydford, Canterbury, Redhill, and Tetbury.

I've also made a number of visits to Kibworth to visit Mum in The Knoll care home, where I'm happt to report she's making good progress and has been drawing a bit of late.

So in this whole 2 months I've been able to manage about seven days clearing out the office and loading it into storage and, to be honest, you wouldn't think I'd done a thing. There is so much still to do that I've had to beg Gerry for another fortnight in which to do it (while also finishing the artwork on my desk). So, before I rush on, let's look at the breakdown of how long Joseph actually took to do.

Script - 23 pages written and laid out Sept 10 - 14 (average 4.6 pages per day)

Art - 23 pages pencilled & inked Sept 26 - 28, Oct 9 - 18 (average 2 pages per day)

Colouring - 23 pages coloured Oct 21 - 31 (average 2.5 pages per day)

So, were I to do nothing but this for a living (and dear reader I once did that, many moons ago) I could produce a 23 page comic every 28 days. If that eventuality comes, the first thing I shall be delegating is the colouring. Now, back to work.

Saturday, 3 November 2018
Hamster Battle Machine Gun -
comics by kids

October has been the quietest
month for Comic Art Masterclasses
of the whole year, surprisingly. Not
that I wasn't stupidly busy with
Denmark and Joseph. So the few
I've done have had to wait till now
to be collected together, topped up
with the above pair, from Foulford
Primary in Cowdenbeath, at the

start of November. I'm rather
chuffed with the cover for Hamster
Battle Machine Gun. A tribute to
which classic comic cover?
(Answer below).

Manchester Literary Festival had
me back, but only for one (sellout
class), and Avonmouth Community
Centre had me over, again for just
the one session. Whatever, we
made some cracking comics. And
of course What Do Pigs... is an

homage to which classic movie? Answer below, if you needed it.

October saw a record proportion of one-off classes, with these from Putney and Sutton Coldfield being more of the same. I'm not saying two classes in a day isn't knackering, but I'm happy to do it.

The celebrities these groups chose for my demonstration strip (which we skipped for the YMCA class to give them more drawing time) were Donald Trump, Kim Jong Un (twice), David Walliams, and most original of the month, Angus Young of AC/DC.

And the tribute covers were based on...

Blazing Combat, a legendary front cover painting by Frank Frazetta from 1965. And...
Citizen Kane, obviously.

Sunday, 4 November 2018
Doctor Who Tsurungdngrumdung Dung - some thoughts

Ever watched a Doctor Who episode where you guessed what the plot twists might be, and they went ahead and didn't bother doing any?
(Spoilers ahoy)

The Doctor is clutching her side in pain.
My thought: The system has rearranged her organs in human configuration not Time Lord, so she's going to have to do an operation on herself to make room for her second heart.
Chibnall's solution: We don't mention her pain again, it just gets better.

There's a clock-ticking time-bomb sense of urgency.

My thought: This will drive the drama and we'll do everything really fast

Chibnall: The lead characters will stop and chat, for absolute ages, really slowly

There's a guy who's about to give birth.

My thought: He's going to do a warrior-like ritual, childbirth being a macho rite of passage for the men of his race.

Chibnall: He's an archetypal woman giving birth, like in Casualty.

The alien out of Lilo and Stitch only green eats spaceship.

My thought: He eats the self destruct mechanism

Chibnall: He eats the self destruct mechanism

My next thought: But then it turns out that this makes him mad and so he's about to eat the rest of the ship double fast, so with great regret The Doctor ejects him

Chibnall: With no regret The Doctor ejects him

There's a famous space pilot who's lying about her illness

My thought: The illness is a bad heart which will be okay as long as she doesn't use the body-linked controls. She only reveals this while she's in mid-rescue and it's too late.

Chibnall: She explains it almost immediately then dies, as you were expecting

The ship has to fly through an asteroid belt

My thought: We see the ship flying through an asteroid belt, which will be exciting

Chibnall: Let's not bother with exciting, eh?

My further thought in the asteroid belt: Just when you think they're safe, there's a big object heading towards them that shouldn't be there. It's one of the Junk Planets (seen at start) spinning out of kilter. And now it's heading for them, the pilot's just died, there's no escape. But why has it changed course, and what can they do?

The solution: The Pting landed on that planet when we ejected it, and has changed its course by eating its core out. Just as the planet's about to hit us, we see the Pting emerging from the junk and, seconds before collision, he eats the last bit of junk and the planet flies apart. We sail home safely.

There's a bomb on the junk planet.
My thought: We find out who put it there and why
Chibnall: Ha ha, yes that would be… nah can't be arsed.

If I'm so clever, why don't I write a Doctor Who episode?

Friday, 9 November 2018
Nugget Munchers - comics by kids in Northumberland

So, can we guess which comic I'm parodying here, on the front cover of the comic produced with kids in Prudhoe in Northumberland? Of course you can, too easy (answer below). Here we see the fruits of a three day run at schools in Northumberland, organised brilliantly again by Gil Pugh of the Hexham Book Festival. I visited six schools in three days, the second example above being from Ovingham, the school with the excellent art teacher Neil Cole, whose newly opened Sci Fi Museum in Allendale was featured on Netflix's Amazing Interiors and is something I look forward to checking out on a future visit.

The beauty of these comics, which the kids take away at the end of each session, is that they look great, no matter how mixed or problematic the classes might be. Not that I'd point a finger at either of these groups, in Morpeth and Ponteland, but it's always made clear in advance that I can work with a maximum of 30 pupils at a time (and I had a contract for these schools saying I'd have 20 in each group), so it was slightly harder going when I found myself trying to work with a group of 36, with only the minimum two hours to 'do' them in. (I do a caricature of every kid in the class, so every child over the odds adds minutes to the time we need). I'm also not a qualified teacher, so the school that left me alone in charge of a class of some the more struggling learners of Year 6 (who needed to be told to shut up every 30 seconds) shall remain nameless.

Northumberland retains a system of Middle Schools, which is where I

was mostly working this week, so you have the odd experience of years 5 to 8 in the same school. Is was it years 6 to 9? Do you know, after half a dozen visits to the area now, I've still not worked it out. Anyway, they were all lovely, these from Cramlington and Bedlington.

The celebrities these six groups chose to star in my demonstration strip were Ali A (a Youtuber m'ud), Daniel Radcliffe, Kanye West, Craig Revel Horwood, David Beckham, and Elvis Presley. A pleasingly diverse range of suggestions, all the more impressive since Simon Cowell and/or Donald Trump were among the names called out in almost every group (I get four suggestions from the room then they select a favourite) and got knocked out in the elimination process. This hardly ever happens.

And the classic comic being parodied was of course...

Sunday, 18 November 2018
"You've got your work cut out here mate" - moving out

And so it was that, on Saturday November 17th, Hev and I finally cleared out of my office on Copse Road, leaving it in an amazingly good state. Hev's work on cleaning mould and insects from the windows and hoovering 16 years of muck from the carpets cannot be understated.

Having been given two months notice at the start of September, it's been a running joke between the two of us that, no matter how much we've cleared out, every time we come into the office we can imagine someone seeing it for the first time saying "Blimey, you've got your work cut out here mate". It was a Sisyphean task but by golly we did it.

Underneath the junk accumulated in my office since I moved in in 2002 were mountains of magazines which, now they've been put into storage, are going to find themselves new homes via eBay. Already the Venue magazines, Private Eyes and Comics Internationals have gone into the paper recycling. The nagging fear that some may have collectibility or, dare I think it, actual commercial value is the only reason I've saved so many into the storage unit. But next to go will be a collection of Doctor Who Adventures complete with toys (which it seems go for about 99p only, so a job lot looms there), Q and Empire magazines, NMEs, then the various 1000s of comics & random magazine that I have

pre-war wooden bookshelf that came from Auntie Kate's house at least 30 years ago, the white filing cabinet that used to be in my childhood bedroom, and a wooden leaf table that was in the office when I arrived. To the tip, or rather the re-use and re-cycle area, have gone five self-assembly six-foot-tall bookshelves that used to line the wall of Mark's and my office above the Midland Bank on Sixways, a Hygena QA Labrenza bookshelf which was in the office when I arrived and which had a bow in the top of it even when I arrived, and two metal strongbox files whose drawers were labelled, among other things, "Immunology". Where they'd come from originally is anyone's guess.

somehow amassed. Why the hell do I have a year's worth of Heat magazine? What was I thinking in the 1990s?

I remember what an achievement it was when, way back at the start of September, we found our storage unit and delivered the first car full of boxes. Well, all I can say is I hope there's nothing in that first layer that I need to get my hands on in a hurry. Because...

This is how it looks today. Somewhere under there is the kitchen table that used to live in Kibworth and has come with us from Leicester to Wrington to Clevedon to my office and now to supporting piles of boxes. There are also two black metal bookshelves that started life in the office I used to share with Mark, a

Hev's sculptures are a bulky, but surprisingly light, part of the load in the storage unit. But it's the magazines and paperwork that form by far the greatest load. How much we've spent on fold-up storage boxes from Argos I shudder to think. The reason it's taken so long to get out - a fortnight longer than my notice allowed - was simply how long it physically took to put everything into boxes and to perform triage on it all. What went to the tip, what went in a box,

and what do I have to keep close to hand in order to try working from home. Having done the artwork for Joseph in a hotel room in Denmark, and coloured my last half dozen jobs on a laptop in various hotel rooms, I'm pretty sure I'll manage working from home for a while, but quite what I'll do about filming Socks videos, and indeed recording new songs, is a mystery. The keyboard, the green screen, and the physical space in which to stick up the green screen and film, are now in a storage unit in Bristol. The Socks even recorded a special farewell to the place in which they've filmed all their studio videos over the last dozen years.

So a new era begins, with a couple of Christmas cards to finish artworking, and more school visits (and a corporate video don'tcha know) taking me around the country (and to Dublin later today) so much I doubt I'll notice the lack of an office for a while yet. What will the future hold? Let us see.

Tuesday, 20 November 2018
Milk, Muffins & Machine guns - comics by kids

A little bit of travelling for this clutch of comics, produced with pupils in my Comic Art Masterclasses, began with a two day visit to Pontefract Library, where pupils were brought in from various primary schools. Pontefract, as everyone knew except me, means

Broken Bridge, and the history of the name is fascinating. Google it. Googling the meme "He Needs Some Milk" is far less edifying, and something one wouldn't expect Year 6s to be so knowledgable about.

I believe Yeah Man may be meme too, but I'm happy to remain ignorant of its derivation. Delightfully, the second of these

Pontefractian suggestions was the sort of flight of imagination by a youngster that makes these comics so worthwhile. When they just parrot the same phrases as each other - which is the definition of memes, obviously - it can get a bit depressing. Year 8, I find, are the worst for it.

Speak of angels and you hear their wings, these were Year 7s and 8s (or First and Second Years as they call them) at Clongowes Wood College in Clane, near Dublin. The first school in Ireland to have me over, and to which I've returned a good few times now. Alumni include James Joyce, Nick Hewer, U2's manager, and Michael Leary of Ryanair. So we got a higher class of meme from this lot, winding up with some sort of rude remix about which I don't wish to know.

The celebrities these 6 groups chose to star in my demonstration strip were Kanye West, Dawyne 'The Rock' Johnson, Ali A, Simon Cowell, Kevin Hart and Michael Jackson. (Either Simon Cowell or Donald Trump was suggested though not chosen in every single class).

Friday, 23 November 2018
I Was Ellie Taylor's First Boyfriend, Apparently

Imagine my surprise when, courtesy of Anne Marie Draycott pointing it out on Twitter, I saw this clip of Ellie Taylor on Live At The Apollo.

"So," she says, in a routine which I can only imagine she's been doing for the last year or more, "I was going out with my first boyfriend, **Kevin Sutherland**."

She goes on to describe my Bart Simpson tattoo and my Liverpool FC bedspread, and how she lost her virginity to them, and to me. Well, I hate to disillusion everybody, but there are clearly two Kevin Sutherlands in the world, what are the chances?

in: Characters, Male Characters, Minor Characters, Sutherland Family

Kevin Sutherland

Kevin Sutherland is the father of Neil and Katie. He is currently
single; his wife having left him. His occupation or employment
status is not directly stated, however it is acknowledged that
he is short of money, with Jay regularly calling him 'pikey',
suggesting that he is most likely unemployed.

Contents [show]

Sexuality ✏ Edit

Unknown

Relationships with other characters ✏ Edit

Kevin Sutherland

Portrayed By: Alex MacQueen

Created By: Damon Beesley and Iain Morris

I would love to find out whether it's
the name of her real first boyfriend,
or whether she attempted to come
up with a made up name and
somehow came up with mine,
rather giving the lie to my imagining
that I have, at least, been heard of
by some of my fellow comedians.
How soon they forget.

This is not, of course, the first time
my name has found its way into a
comedy I had nothing to do with, as
anyone who's familiar with The
Inbetweeners will know.

Yes. As well as being Ellie Taylor's
first boyfriend, I'm also Neil's gay
Dad. I get about a bit.

This bit of name-calling has an
easier explanation, resulting from
the days when Iain Morris and I
worked together on some sitcom

writing a little over 20 years ago.
He created the character Jesper
who went on to be in the sitcom
Yikes It's Jesper, co-written by
myself and Ken Elkes, with
additional material by half a dozen
writers including Iain.

Having staged a couple of
episodes as part of Situations
Vacant, my first attempt at a live
sitcom showcase, we sent Yikes
It's Jesper to the BBC and it got
snapped up by a producer who
knew his onions, the excellent Jon
Rolph. Iain, by this time, had
graduated from University and
gone to work for a series of TV
companies, opting out of the
project, so his character was
written out and the piece renamed
Come Together. It was given a
BBC radio pilot starring Ben Miller,
Arabella Wier, Melanie Hudson and

Kevin Eldon, but amazingly didn't make it to a series.

A decade later Iain had worked his way to the top of the sitcom producing business and co-created The Inbetweeners with his fellow Channel 4 commissioning editor Damon Beesley, and the rest is history. I like to think his inclusion of my name for one of the more heavily-ridiculed characters in the show was affectionate. He hasn't, to date, commented on the matter.

Before he moved on to better things, Iain appeared in a few Sits Vac shows. Here he is starring as a posh rapper in Band For Life, a sitcom whose script was, being honest, no better than its title.

Monday, 26 November 2018
Christmas Cardathon - Teasers

This year I have drawn a record number of Christmas cards for people, and I have to say I'm rather happy with what I've churned out. Obviously it would be wrong to spoil the surprise for anyone who's about to receive this little lot, so I hope you'll be happy with these tiny teasers from the yet-to-be-opened Christmas cards I've had a hand in. Starting with the above excerpt from a mega card, a front-and-back colour spread featuring nearly 100 different representations of the season as suggested by the sender's family and friends. If you're one of that number you're in for a treat.

This one was for a group of friends who are fans of a certain TV show. I don't know if you can make out a rift in time and a classic sonic and console there in the background?

There was a lot of that sort of thing in there.

No surprise whose card this comes from. When you see the full panorama of this mega production, let's see how many people are still able to spot the Bath Comedy Festival Best Joke Award tucked away there in the background.

This card's not actually finished yet. It's for a client for whom I've been drawing the card for more than a decade now. I've got used to the fact that it'll go through a few more changes before it's finished (this is already the fourth version of Santa's face, and he's not even the star of the card.)

UPDATE: What did I say about this card? Since I posted this blog yesterday they've had me redraw Santa's face yet again. Here's the latest version.

Here's the sort of job I love, a client who knows what she wants, writes some funny word play, and keeps my bit of it dead simple. Drawing bags of crisps and Mickey Mouse is my idea of fun.

This isn't strictly a Christmas card, but I drew it last week for an end of year presentation, so let's count it shall we? It's for a school near Dublin that does a golf related event. They're supposed to be famous golfers, but I'll be the first to admit it quite possibly doesn't look like any of them.

Since they've put it online themselves I guess there's no harm

in you seeing this in full. It's the cover art for The Sound Of Thunder podcast's Christmas Special, available as a CD which is whose sleeve this art will be adorning. One of two cards this year that required drawings of both Dickens and Scrooge, what were the chances?

And last but by no means least, a card that's particularly close to my heart, taking a dozen drawings by Mum and assembling them into a finished design, devised by her. You'll love this when you see it.

Anyone else want their Christmas cards drawing? You may have left it too late. But don't forget to get your dibs in for next year. I started this lot back in October.

Tuesday, 4 December 2018
Socks gigs spring 2019

Jan 27 - Big Burns Supper. As part of this festival in Dumfries, we're doing an afternoon show, with the best of our stuff, plus our Burns Night material and, hopefully, the first tryout of material from the new Roll Up! show.

This means we're AVAILABLE FOR BURNS NIGHT (25th) and we're already in Scotland. So if you want us, get in touch pronto Tonto.

Feb 15 & 16 - Leicester Comedy Festival. The first tryouts for the new show, Roll Up!

March 20 - 22 - **Glasgow Comedy Festival**. Three nights of tryouts of the new show, Roll Up!
March 20 & 21 at Dram! and March 22 at Britannia Panopticon Music Hall.

Britannia Panopticon is the historic music hall, sealed up for 70 years and only unveiled at the turn of the century, now preserved as a theatre museum. It's where Stan Laurel first performed and dates back to the Victorian era. Warning: there is no heating, so this gig requires dressing up warm. If you want a cosy show, come to one of the Dram nights.

April 6 - **Socks do Superheroes** at The Rondo Theatre in Bath. A final mini-tour for last year's Award Winning show. Appropriately, since we won the award in Bath, we're returning to Bath Comedy Festival to give them a 90 minute show including Superheroes.
April 12 - **Socks do Superheroes** at The Ropewalk Barton On Humber. 90 minute show.
April 13 - **Socks Do Superheroes** at Artrix in Bromsgrove. 90 minutes show.

June 1 & 2 - Socks Roll Up! at Brighton Fringe.

More gigs to come, stay tuned.

Thursday, 6 December 2018
It's Beginning To Smell A Lot Like Xmas - new song from the Socks

Brand new from the Socks, a Christmas number one if ever we heard one - It's Beginning To Smell A Lot Like Christmas. Click and enjoy. I wrote this just before we went up to Kibworth last Christmas, on Christmas Eve itself I seem to recall, so I had no time to put it online before it went out of date and have sat on it for a year. It actually got a live airing at the Leicester Comedy Festival previews for Superheroes back in February, but sadly I've lost the footage. So, with vocals finally recorded this week and a video shot on Hill Road in Clevedon (I still don't have a studio set up for my green screen), here's the video the world's been waiting for. What's that you say? You want the lyrics? Oh, go on then...

IT'S BEGINNING TO SMELL A LOT LIKE XMAS

It's beginning to smell a lot like Xmas
Because of the brussel sprouts
With potatoes and beans as well
Contributing to the smell
Which let's face it is better in than out

It's beginning to smell a lot like
Xmas
Wafting from every door
And the prettiest sight we know's
When you open the windows
And let it out once more

A string of trumpeting poots from a
bottom that toots
Are the gift of Grandad and Gran
And a couple of si-a-lent ones that
are violent
Seem to have started with Nan
And there's a fog must be the dog
It cannot be human

It's beginning to smell a lot like
Xmas
Everywhere you turn
Is it cabbage or is it leeks?
Whatever it is it reeks
And nobody strike a match cos it'll
burn

It's beginning to smell a lot like
Xmas
It's getting worse, I think you'll find
That the biggest relief will come

When we get to set off home
And leave the smell behind

The kind that get in your face and
the ones you can taste
Are the sort where father excels
But your Mum and your sister will
always insist
that they're blamed on somebody
else
And one of you has followed
through and done a poo as well

It's beginning to smell a lot like
Xmas
Nobody can breathe
And when everyone's had enough
Of the other peoples guff
Then we'll have to leave

Friday, 7 December 2018
The Nativity Comic by Kev F
Sutherland

Monday, 10 December 2018
Doctor Who series 11 Verdict - 5
likes, 5 dislikes

Here, as published in a small run
last year by Bible Society, and
now released online for the first
time, is my comic strip adaptation
of **The Nativity**, in its full 16 page
glory. If you enjoy this and would
like to see more of my humorous
adaptations of Bible stories (eg
adaptations of The Book Of Esther,
Book Of Ruth, and the stories of
Joseph, Rahab, and Jael Wife Of
Heber, all of which are waiting in
the wings to be unleashed on the
world) please contact Bible Society,
my publishers, telling them how
much you want to see them. Every
bit of feedback helps. Now, enjoy,
and a Merry Christmas to you all...

Well, that was fun wasn't it? No, I'm
not saying I loved the series,
indeed you can prepare yourself for
some good hating ahead, but I
loved the fact that everybody was
talking about it.

I say everybody, obviously I live in
a particular bubble of the sort of
folks who talk about Doctor Who all
the time, and whose most exciting
Christmas present this year will be
Blu Rays of the first Peter Davison
season (which, for the record, I
hated at the time and have
watched with nothing but
embarrassment since). But I have
been delighted to find lots more
people - in particular kids in
schools - who have been aware of

Doctor Who this year, and in some way engaged by it.

A lot of this, true, has been tabloids and twaddle merchants banging on about the stories being "too PC". Though, as Mandeep Gill pointed out in an interview, PC stands for Politically Correct, and "how can something be too correct?" QED. And there's been heightened attention drawn to the fact that Jodie's the first woman in the lead role, but most sensible people got over that fact by, oh, July 2017. Didn't they?

So I loved my favourite telly show* (*I'll qualify that when I give my rundown on my Top TV of the year, and you shouldn't hold your breath in the hope of Doctor Who taking the top spot) being watched by lots more people than in recent years, and lots of them being kids and families. This was clear when I worked with kids in my Comic Art Masterclasses, among the sweetest being a 6 year old kid who described to me the whole story so far in lovely childlike detail, including how her Tardis was her Ghost Monument. That's what I was waiting to hear.

But what did I personally think of

the series overall? Here are some likes and dislikes.

LIKES

Personality and characters

I've never been silent on the fact that I'm a Russell T Davies fan. He created and show-ran my favourite 4 years of Doctor Who, and I find the episodes from his run endlessly rewatchable. My biggest criticism of Moffat's run when it started was that I didn't relate to the characters. This is the part that Chris Chibnall has got right. Those moments between Graham, Grace, Ryan and Yaz have been the backbone of the series, and the one consistent thread that gets my vote every time.

Twitter has been alive with Yaz &

me loved his Missy and Cybermen stories, and the comics reader in me appreciated the ambition of his River Song and other story arcs, reminiscent as they were of the Alan Moore books we both grew up with, the clever-cleverness alienated newcomers to the series.

The Doctor's girlfriend moments, and Graham and Ryan's Grandad stuff. This is good TV drama writing and has been what's led me to describe this series as "Call The Midwife with special effects". In a good way.

The topping and tailing of Arachnids In The UK with the scenes where The Doctor nearly loses then wins back her "fam" are the most effective such moments of character writing since Donna, Rose and Wilf.

Non clever-cleverness

I used to be the biggest Steven Moffat fan, especially when he was out-shining RTD during RTD's own seasons. But when Moffat became show runner, and his love of puzzles, complexity, gag-driven wordplay, and fanboy-pleasing self-referential indulgence took over, it became harder and harder to warm to his stories. While the fanboy in

Chris Chibnall may be many things, but clever-clever isn't two of them.

Chibnall has kept it simple, and when that works, it really works. Every one of these episodes, whether you liked them or not, can be easily described to friends the next day. Every one is "that one where", and they've had a great level of quotability to them too. There has only been one episode (It Takes You Away) where any viewer would be left going "what just happened?" and having to explain it to a dozy relative or half-watching mate. And even then, that's cos the story was a bit bonkers, not cos you had to "keep up". When it helps accessibility and new viewers to join the party, I'm all for keeping it simple.

No old monsters

This was a brave move and a good one. Treat new viewers as new friends, make the series stand on its own. Russell T Davies almost did this with his first season, though he had to include the Daleks but managed to create mostly his own new enemies. Moffat's first season had pretty well every old villain there had ever been chucked in there. For Chibnall to manage a whole run with only new characters and challenges is admirable. If only they'd all been... but we'll come to that.

Scheduling, presentation, promotion

Sunday night was an excellent choice, the best scheduling choice since 2004's "let's bring the series back." Abandoning the pre-credit sequence was a nice touch. The 10 episodes only was a shame, for those of us who greedily wanted more, but good on him for making the choice and sticking with it. And the promotions, leaking the minimum amount of spoilage in advance, were excellently handled. Even the "Glass Ceiling" trailer was fine by me.

The PR for this series, from the team's instagram movies and tweets to all the press calls, have stood out and done the show

favours. I cringe when I recall the announcement of Capaldi as the Doctor, way too OTT, and that Doctor Live Afterparty show they did with One Direction and the cast, shudder. Jodie Whittaker has been the best Doctor Who in interviews since David Tennant (sorry Matt and Peter, but she just has).

And that theme tune

Best theme tune since the 1970s. I liked the 2005 orchestration, but this is just so much more alien and futuristic. Love it.

DISLIKES

Lack of visual imagination

One thing the RTD era will always have is visually memorable villains and supporting characters. From

Fonzie. Spiders, but big. The Absorbaloff, but small. Aliens in black leather again. Delivery bots (OK, they were good). Mud monsters from The Curse Of Fenric, but more monotone. A talking frog (OK, that was good too). And the alien in black leather again, who I will confess did have interesting teeth stuck in his face.

But a guy with teeth on his face, delivery bots and a frog on a chair aren't going to be the toyshop smashes that the Cybermen helmet and the remote controlled Daleks were. They're not even going to give The Face Of Boe a run for his money. (Yes, I still have a Face Of Boe, worth nothing on eBay I've found.)

the Slitheen and Lady Cassandra (the stretched-skin woman?), through Weeping Angels and Clockwork Robots, to the best ever designs of Daleks and Cybermen, Russell T Davies ensured there were great designs to make into toys for Christmas. Moffat arguably gave us less memorable designs, though you can't deny he was trying with The Silence, The Spinners (not, not the folk band, I mean those whirly-headed things in The Beast Below), and the worst ever designs of Daleks and Cybermen.

What has Chibnall given us? Household objects but blown up big.

Electric cables that wriggle and an alien in black leather. Shreds of paper that wriggle. A time-travelling

Lack of drama

I went into The Tsuranga Conundrum in some detail in this blog (and don't get me started on stupid titles like this and The Battle Of Ranskoor Av Kolos) so I won't repeat myself. Suffice it to say I'm disappointed in Chibnall's dramatic writing. We believe in the characters, that bit he's nailed. But then they get into situations which they explain and re-explain every single time, with exposition taking the place of action at every opportunity. It's like he missed the Show Don't Tell module of a creative writing course.

This has resulted in every episode coming across more like a radio drama than a TV show. There has been so much standing around - in space ship control rooms which all have their operating system in the middle of the room, like a Tardis but with less imagination - and talking through situations. And how many times did the nature of the problem and/or the solution just pop into The Doctor's head? Rather than being a surprise, a discovery, a twist, a revelation, or the work of one of the characters? Not often enough.

It is this fault that has been my biggest complaint of the series. Moffat may have been too clever-clever, but when you got to the solution of one of his twist storylines, at least you'd get some Keyser Soke-like satisfaction (eg The Empty Child, Silence In The Library, Missy is The Master etc). With Chibnall, whatever you expect is going to happen is exactly what then happens. Often with the help of the "Get Out Of Jail Free" overuse of a Sonic Screwdriver.

And slow bloody motion! How much more slow motion did we have to go through before we all started crying out "wait a minute, this 45 minute show only has 30 minutes of script!"

Lack of ambition

By the middle of this series I was full of praise. Chibnall had set up the best start of a series since Russell T Davies. He was even following the same template as RTD's first season. Episode 4 had a title that riffed on a pop song (Aliens Of London / Arachnids In The UK), there was an episode title with 4 letters, the first 3 if which were Ros, and most importantly it made you believe in the central characters, rooted in their hometown, and now we were off to enjoy the ambitious stories.

With RTD it came with Dalek, then Fathers Day, then The Empty Child, then the brilliant finale. The best TV episodes Doctor Who had ever seen. RTD found great new writers and broke new ground in storytelling. He kept doing it himself, with stories like Love & Monsters, and Midnight, stories you couldn't tell anywhere else. Moffat did this too, bringing in writers like Simon Nye, Richard Curtis, Neil Gaiman, Jamie Mathieson, and Frank Cottrell-Boyce, and giving them a creative carte blanche. To mixed results, but at least they tried.

Chibnall managed this once, with Malorie Blackman's Rosa. And it's possible that Kerblam and It Takes You Away will be seen kindly as such standout episodes. But was anything trying to do stuff that

you'd never seen on TV before? I'm not sure.

The same damn things over and over again

How many times was there a 'thing' on the floor in a clearing in a forest? How many times did The Doctor stand her gang round in a circle and explain things? How many spaceships did we get sucked into whose console was in the middle of the room? How many villains spoke in cliched dialogue like a 1970s kids TV show, usually with their voice modulated to sound deeper? How many times did the Doctor suddenly remember who these aliens were and then explain their entire history? How many times did the whole gang and some hangers on walk down a big dirt track in the middle of a quarry/desert/bit of Punjab/junkyard while the camera panned down to show objects in the foreground.

I'm sure someone is already putting together a compilation of all the bits of this season of Doctor Who that just looked the same as each other, if they don't get too bored.

And no new series in 2019?

Monday, 10 December 2018
Top TV of 2018 - Lost It, Also Rans, & Hast Thou Got Crops In Jethro?

I am reminded of the Woody Allen joke. The food here is awful. Yes, and such small portions.

I know everyone will disagree with everyone else's opinions, I just wanted to get mine down for the record. And, as I've said a million times before, if I'm so clever why aren't I writing Doctor Who? I should put up or shut up, but for the time being here I am doing a bit of neither. Allons-y.

HAST THOU GOT CROPS IN, JETHRO?

Winners of the **Hast Thou Got Crops In Jethro?** Prize (for shows that shoehorn life lessons in in place of drama. Last year's top three were The A Word, Loves Lies & Records and The Good Place)

3) Come Home - The wife walks out on Christopher Eccleston and the kids and he does his usual pained face, this time with a Norther Irish accent. Moral: People are complicated.

2) Collateral - A pizza guy gets shot and something something immigration and er politics and lesbian vicars and something

something. Moral: Life is complicated.

1) Butterfly - Kid is transgender. Moral: You can never over-explain things too much in an ITV drama.

LOST IT

A dozen shows we lost interest in, or who lost the plot in 2018 (in no particular order)

Plebs 4 (new casting and location, not the show it was)
This Country 2 (novelty's worn off)
Humans 3 (lasted only a couple of eps)
Press (soapy, one ep)
Wanderlust (one ep)
Hard Sun (one ep, it was laughable)
No Offence 3 (gave up halfway through ep 5)
Black Earth Rising (3 eps, just not gripping, though very worthy)
Lost In Space (half a dozen, don't know why we watched that many)

Black Lightning (drifted two thirds through, was enjoying it, spread thin)
Orange Is The New Black 6 (gave up after 5 eps, sub par after previous series)
Walking Dead (didn't even start the new series - we have the whole thing staring at us from the recorder, they're going to get wiped unseen)

BUBBLING UNDER

Shows we have watched and enjoyed that didn't make the Top 25 chart.

Bobs Burgers, Brooklyn 99, Young Offenders, Urban Myths, The Repair Shop, Mrs Wilson, Bodyguard, Vic & Bob's Big Night Out, Top Of The Pops 1985/6, Only Connect, Strictly Come Dancing, Eastenders, Richard Osman's House Of Games

So which shows made my **Top 25 TV Shows of 2018**? Read on…

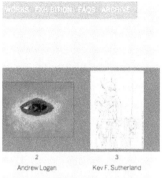

2
Andrew Logan

3
Kev F. Sutherland

1202
Heather Tweed

1203
Phil Sofer

Tuesday, 11 December 2018
Hev & Kev in RCA Secrets
Check me out, front and centre on the front page of the RCA Secrets website this year. What do you mean you've never heard of it? For shame. Look, here's one of Hev's entries...

That's just one of Hev's three cards in this year's RCA Secrets, I have three in there as well. And is that Michael Bartlett, to the right, the same man who was head of my 4D Department at Exeter in the 1980s? It would be brilliant if it was.

The way RCA Secrets works is that a number of artists, by invitation don't cha know, are given three postcards each, to decorate as they see fit. These cards are then displayed, anonymously, and sold on opening night, with all moneys

going to the support of the Royal College Of Art. Here's an interview I did with RCA Secrets back in 2011.

Artists who've entered this year include Jeremy Dellar, Grayson Perry, Nick Park, Maggi Hambling, Ridley Scott and hundreds more. And, of course, Kev Sutherland and Heather Tweed.

Both Heather's and my cards were produced during her exhibition at Christmas Steps back in September. Heather's are prints based on Lulu, the circus performer she's doing work on, and my cards were simply biro drawings of the gallery and Hev's exhibition.

I hope our cards have gone to good homes. I've only ever met one person who's ever bought my

card, I suppose statistically it's unlikely that I should even have managed that. She was a teacher at The Brit School, as I recall. Hmm, I wonder if my niece Shona has met her. We should compare notes. Anyhoo, here's to being invited to be in RCA Secrets again next time, and congratulations to all the buyers who got a surprisingly valuable card by a top artist. Commiserations to whoever got me again.

Tuesday, 11 December 2018
Merry Christmas from Mum

Merry Christmas from Mum, Corral Sutherland. As you probably know she's not well and is in a care home in Kibworth, so we've helped her out finishing off the card (all the drawings are hers though) and sending them. A lucky few have the printed card, but she wants everyone to see it, and please print it out and stick it on the wall if you can.

Merry Christmas, love from Mum, Jude, Heather, me and all the extended family.

Here are some of the preparatory stages that went into the completing of the card. Mum had a couple of stabs at drawing the final

Merry Christmas from Kev F & The Scottish Falsetto Socks

Hopefully everyone who's getting this through the post has already had it, so here for the world at large is this year's official Christmas card from Kev F the comic artist, and the Scottish Falsetto Sock Puppet Theatre.

five groups of characters.

The original Maids A Milking and piper, from back in September.

A first draft of the card, from September, which I'm glad we didn't go with. It's my layout and, ouch, it hurts my eyes. What was I thinking?

Mum's revised Maids A Milking, with which she was a lot happier. And in case you never saw her original Twelve Days Of Christmas cards, which began in 2013, here's how the first one looked.

Just to remind you that, when she was on top form, Mum's draughtsmanship knocks spots off anything I've ever managed to do. Merry Christmas all.

On there you'll see just a fraction of the comics I've produced in this year's Comic Art Masterclasses, you can see my major comic productions Woman Of The Bible and Joseph, you can see the Socks' with their Superheroes comic commemorating this year's hit show, and you can see their award that they won for Best Joke at this year's Bath Comedy Festival. You can also probably spot my appearance on The Apprentice, which was my moment of televisual glory this year.

And since you're on, how about a special treat for you. Here's the original version of the card that was almost going to go to the printers before I decided it frankly didn't say "Christmas" enough. Can you spot the difference?

Merry Christmas everyone, and a

happy new year when it comes.

(TOP SECRET sneak preview - now don't tell anyone you've seen this cos they're not out yet, but for those of you who've scrolled down this far, here is Hev & Kev's 2018 Christmas card - and it's in 3D. You'll need a 3D viewer to see it properly (sorry we can't send one to everyone. But if you have one, the classic Victorian kind which

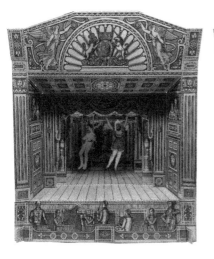 

holds the image about three inches from your eyes and has two little eyeholes with lenses in to focus with, then download this image to your phone - swipe and it should copy - fill the screen with it portaitways, and voila! Let your eyes focus and, bingo, it's in 3D. I for one am very impressed. All Hev's idea, using her Pollocks toy theatre and images from her Lulu book and exhibition. I just helped with the execution. Enjoy)

Here, should you be interested, are my some past cards from...

2017 - Kev F comic card, the Socks' card
2016 - Kev F comic card, the Socks' Shakespeare card
2015 - Kev F comic card, the

Socks' Minging Detectives card
2014 - teasers for mine & the Socks' cards, I failed to put the finished things online!
2013 - Kev F schools card, the Socks don't seem to have had one
2012 - Hev & Kev's fairytale card (a classic, above), Kev F schools card,
2011 - Hev & Kev's and the Socks cards
2010 - Hev & Kev's card (below), and Kev F comic card

Wednesday, 12 December 2018
Band Aid 1974

DAVID ESSEX It's Christmas time, there's no need to be afraid
At Christmas time we let in light and we banish shade

ELTON JOHN And in our world of plenty, we can spread a smile of joy
Throw your arms around the world at Christmas time

Drums - **COZY POWELL**

ROD STEWART But say a prayer, pray for the other ones, at Christmas time it's hard

ROGER DALTREY But when you're having fun, there's a world outside your window

GARY GLITTER And it's a world of dread and fear

BRIAN CONNOLLY of SWEET Where the only water flowing is the bitter sting of tears

LES GRAY of MUD & **BRYAN FERRY** And the Christmas bells that ring there are the clanging chimes of doom

NODDY HOLDER Well tonight thank God it's them instead of you

DAVID BOWIE And there won't be snow in Africa this Christmas time
The greatest gift they'll get this year is life

LULU, GILBERT O'SULLIVAN & SUZI QUATRO Where nothing ever grows, no rain nor rivers flow

ROY WOOD & MARC BOLAN Do they know it's Christmas time at all?

PAUL McCARTNEY Here's to you **THE WHO** Raise a glass for everyone

JOHN LENNON Here's to them **THE WHO** Underneath that burning sun

McCARTNEY, LENNON, HARRISON & STARR Do they know it's Christmas time at all?

CHOIR including **THE BAY CITY ROLLERS, THE THREE DEGREES, THE FACES, SHOWADDYWADDY, LYNSEY DEPAUL, THE RUBETTES, PAPER LACE and THE WOMBLES** Feed the world - let them know it's Christmas time

Monday, 17 December 2018
Suck Your Bum In - the last kids comics of the year

And, with these two comics by kids at North Tawton Primary in Devon, my Comic Art Masterclasses come to an end for 2018. December's usually a quiet month, for obvious reasons, so this was a nice pair of strong covers to go out with. The first group's teacher wanted a historic theme, and got it. The second group, luckily, couldn't spell blew.

Two classes in a day, one in Knaresborough, one in Ripon. And, by dint of the fact that I'm writing this blog a fortnight later, I can remember nothing about either class. Looks like they were fun. The phrase "suck your bum in" is a thing I say to get kids to tuck their chairs in so I can get past. And now it's been immortalised, hallelujah.

This comic cover and flipchart are from an afternoon class in Resolven in South Wales (followed by a Socks gig later). It was the day after Stan Lee dies, hence the commemorative flipchart and, pleasingly, their choice for the celebrity in the demonstration strip.

I've done two classes now with kids for the Cleft Lip and Palate Association, putting together material for a Clapa comic, to be fully properly printed with the kids strips themselves forming the majority of the magazine, finished off by me. This was part of that, from a session in London.

The celebs five of these six groups chose to star in my demonstration strip were Ant McPartlin, Declan Donnelly (twice), Stan Lee and Simon Cowell (we dispensed with the demo strip for the Clapa group because of timing). Which means I can now draw up the final list of The Most Popular Celebrity As Chosen By Kids in 2018...

Monday, 17 December 2018

2018's Most Popular Celebrity with schoolkids is..?

This year my visits to schools took me to Switzerland twice and to all points of the British Isles. Yes even the Isle Of Wight. As always in my Comic Art Masterclasses I ask the kids to come up with a celebrity to draw in my demonstration strip. I get four suggestions from the room, then do a quick knockout between them so we end up with what should be the room's favourite. It seems to keep them focussed on the strip I then draw, and gives me the opportunity for a bit of improv around the character, which is always fun. The celebrities they choose get mentioned somewhere on each cover.

So who did they choose in 2018? Here are the results.

ONCERS - only chosen the one time

Anthony Joshua
Ariana Grande
Barry Scott (Cillit Bang)
Bear Grylls
Boris Johnson
Bruce Willis
Craig Revel Horwood
Dan TDM
Daniel Radcliffe
David Bowie
Eddie Redmayne
Gigi Hadid (a model)
Harry Styles

Hugh Jackman
Jake Paul (a Youtuber)
Jeff Kinney (Diary Of A Wimpy Kid)
JK Rowling
John Cena
John Travolta
Jon Bon Jovi
Justin Bieber
Mary Berry
Olly Murrs
Pablo Escobar
Paul Walker (Fast & Furious)
Prince Harry
Roald Dahl
Robbie Williams
Robert Downey Jr
Selena Gomez
Stephen Hawking
Stan Lee
Taylor Swift
The Pope
Theresa May
Tom Holland
Tom Jones

Usain Bolt
Vladimir Putin
Will Ferrell

…of which my favourite stand-out
original suggestions have to be…

Angus Young of ACDC
Gilbert O'Sullivan
Geoff Nutkins (aviation artist)
William The Conqueror
Sir Isaac Newton
Bob Ross
Dracula

CHOSEN TWICE:
Ali A
Chris Pratt
Elvis Presley
Gordon Ramsay
Harry Hill
Johnny Depp
Kanye West
Kevin Hart
Lionel Messi

7th PLACE - chosen 3 times each

Ant McPartlin (2017 once)
Barack Obama (2017 6th/5, 2016
5th/6, 2015 8th/4)
Beyonce (2017 twice, 2016 once)
Cristiano Ronaldo (2017 3rd/8,
2016 11th/3, 2015 4th/8)
Tom Cruise (2017 once, 2016
once)

6th PLACE - chosen 4 times each

David Attenborough (2017 once)
David Beckham (2017 not chosen,
2016 7th/5)
Dwayne 'The Rock' Johnson
(2017 twice)

5th PLACE - chosen 5 times each

David Walliams (2017 5th/6, 2016
not chosen, 2015 7th/5)
The Queen (2017 5th/6, 2016 5th/
6, 2015 5th/7)

4th PLACE - chosen 6 times

Declan Donnelly (2017 once)

THIRD PLACE - chosen 8 times
each

Kim Kardashian (2017 4th/7, 2016
4th/7, 2015 3rd/10)
Kim Jong Un (2017 not chosen,

2016 once)
Michael Jackson (2017 7th /4, 2016 11th/3, 2015 2nd/12)

SECOND PLACE - chosen 16 times

Simon Cowell
(2017 2nd/11; 2016 2nd/20; 2015, 14 & 13 1st Place)

And the **WINNER**, for the third year running:

Donald Trump - chosen 30 times (2017 42 times, 2016 25 times, 2015 twice, before that he'd never been mentioned)

Thanks for joining in with this futile and not-even-quasi-scientific study. We look forward to reporting back on more such trivia in 2019.

Tuesday, 18 December 2018
My Top TV of 2018 (Part 2, 25 - 11)

26) A special mention for **The Apprentice**, only cos I was in it. It's a staple, and one we enjoy. But one of the genuine best TV shows of the year? Sorry Lord Siralan.

25) **Disenchantment** (Netflix)
Matt Groening's fairytale animation erred on the side of fairytale telling and kept forgetting to keep the comedy in there, especially towards the end. No Futurama, but fun.

24) **Peaky Blinders** (BBC, on Netflix)
We came to this a few years after everyone else and, three seasons in, now understand what everyone was going on about.

anyone's chart.

23) The Good Place (Netflix)
Seasons 1 and 2 were excellent, but season 3 is less so. These charts are hard to compile when you watch all three win the same year.

22) Vanity Fair (ITV)
An excellent new adaptation, getting the most of the comedy and drama in Thackeray. Definitely wins best 19th Century period drama of the year.

21) Mum 2 (BBC)
Still brilliant, a quiet comedy gem that will be a delight to revisit for years to come.

20) Inside No 9 (BBC)
A fourth excellent series may not have been as strong as their earlier ones, but the live Halloween episode earns them a place in

19) Preacher 3 (Amazon)
Suffering a little from the spend-a-season-in-one-location trap that made Walking Dead so boring, Preacher still has more novel ideas than most shows. And I did love the comics.

18) Feud: Bette & Joan (FX/BBC)
The first of four shows in my chart made by FX, which I didn't realise until I double-checked. They are punching above their weight. These award-winning impersonations were to die for.

17) Upstart Crow 3 (BBC)
After a year doing Shakespeare with the Socks, I still remain the person who admits liking this series. Ended on a bit of a downer, but hopefully the Christmas episode will save it.

16) Black Mirror 4 (Netflix)
Diverse, dark, and wearing its big

budget on its sleeve, these dystopian sci fi stories did what I wish Doctor Who would do. A few too many had the same "brain thing stuck to the temple" theme to them, but that's a small quibble for such amazing imaginative fiction.

15) **Better Call Saul 3** (Netflix)
And then nothing happened. Such mastery of the screen, to be able to spin so little action out so well, but by golly they do. Sooooooo well.

14) **Handmaids Tale 2** (C4/Hulu)
Not getting any lighter, and still doing things in TV storytelling that no-one else has done, an adaptation of a 30 year old book continues to amaze.

13) **The Crown 2** (Netflix)
It suffers from being on at the start of the year. If it had just been on, I'd probably put it at number one. Being divided into such perfect stand alone films this will be a delight to revisit. As it is, let me join the BAFTAs in not giving it the praise it deserves by squeezing it out of the top ten.

12) **GLOW 2** (Netflix)
Such good fun, and continuing to mine the characters of its wide range of diverse characters, the

lady wrestlers are better TV now than lady wrestlers can possibly have been in real life.

11) **Talking Pictures TV** (Freeview channel 81, Virgin channel 445)
It's not a show, it's a channel and if I haven't raved about it to you yet, just corner me at a party sometime. Showing old films, largely British, it became our have-on-in-the-background channel this year. We wake up to it, fill gaps with it. And, every now and again, watch an entire movie on it. The best wallpaper on TV, and the channel that's had me going to Google most often to find out whatever happened to the actor we're looking at.

And my **Top Ten** TV of 2018? Thanks for asking, it look like this…

Wednesday, 19 December 2018
My Top TV of 2018 (Part 3 The Top Ten)

10) **Doctor Who** series 11 (BBC)
It's become something of a tradition for my favourite telly show to come into my chart at number ten. I want it to be higher, but this year it was too disappointing for that to happen. I liked a lot, I disliked a lot. I've written a blog about it. And I won't have to worry where it places again for another two years.

9) **The End Of The F**ing World** (C4 / Netflix)
A hidden gem of a murder mystery based on a graphic novel. We missed it when first shown, then caught it on Netflix. Staying small and unpredictable made it a winner. And a tremendous soundtrack curated by Graham

Coxon.

8) **A Very English Scandal** (BBC)
I loves me a bit of Russell T Davies and his adaptation of the true story of the Jeremy Thorpe affair was brilliant. Funniest murder show of the year, and by golly there was stiff competition.

7) **Killing Eve** (BBC America)
More funny murder, this time erring on the side of filmic brilliance. If only all spy movies were this clever.

6) **Young Sheldon** (CBS/E4)
I couldn't believe it when this seemed to get no Emmy nominations. The funniest sitcom to come from the States this year, from the mainstream channels (who don't get much of a look in in recent years), it's family friendly

and kind of old fashioned, in a new and perfect way.

5) **Atlanta** (FX)

Brilliant laugh out loud comedy characters, who can turn on a sixpence into dark and pathetic drama. Taking the most surreal and unexpected turns, and unveiling a world that makes you want to have nothing to do with making rap music or ever visiting Atlanta Georgia.

4) **Trust** (FX/BBC)

Simon Beaufoys and Danny Boyle's masterful filmic drama, including an episode entirely in Italian. The most beautiful cinematography of the year and the most unpredictable storyline, given that it was possible to google what really happened.

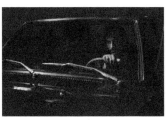

3) **The Assassination of Gianni Versace** (FX/BBC)

Another one where you could google the truth and miss the whole point. Both this and Trust told their story in self-contained episodes, each of which was a film in themselves. By jumping forwards and backwards in time this played the greatest tricks on your expectations. Daniel Criss as Andrew Cunanan is creepiest TV killer of the year, and my pick to play the next Master.

2) **Derry Girls** (C4)

British, or rather Irish, sitcom of the year, this was another treat hidden away in the Channel 4 desert. Quite how one plugs a TV show to the public these days I don't know, but I'm glad we found this by accident then used the magic of Catch Up to, well, catch up. Truly

exceptional. And when it comes to ending a funny show on a sad note, Derry Girls wins hands down.

1) The Marvellous Mrs Maisel (Amazon)

Heavens to Murgatroyd this is amazing. Hev has become a fan of The Gilmore Girls and so is acquainted with Amy Sherman Palladino's writing, but this was a revelation to me. How sharp? How witty? How fast moving? How wide ranging? And how much do we suspend our disbelief when Midge does her stand up, knowing that no stand up has ever been like that, that no audience has every responded like that, that you can't be heard without a microphone like that, that… seriously no-one notices any of those things because The Marvellous Mrs Maisel is so, let's face it, Marvellous. (Oh yeah, the one fault, the Americans can't spell Marvelous.)

So there are my favourites of the year. What did I miss?

Here's to a 2019 of even more televisual fun.

Monday, 24 December 2018
Fannying About The Christmas Tree, live

Here's a treat, one that I'd forgotten existed. A live performance of the Socks' 2017 Christmas song Fannying Around The Christmas Tree, recorded live in Leicester back in February.

I'd uploaded it to Youtube but only shared it with fans who were supporting our Kickstarter campaign. So now, in time for the big day, here it is for everyone to enjoy.

Interesting its title has changed from Fannying Around... to Fannying About... Both titles work I guess, one is truer to the song it's parodying, and one goes slightly better as a way of putting it. Sadly the footage of the whole show disappeared when I had my laptop upgraded in the summer, so a live version of Beginning To Smell A Lot Like Xmas has gone.

Tuesday, 25 December 2018
Merry Christmas from Hev & Kev

Merry Christmas from Hev and Kev. And thanks to Hev's interest in stereoscopy - she did a course about it last year don't cha know, we have a 3D card this year. The image above is the straightforward printed version. Now check this out...

If you have a 3D viewer (either an old fashioned Victorian stereoscope, a Google Cardboard is, I believe, popular with the kids as a VR headset) get this onto your phone and have a look. Impressive eh? And if that doesn't work, try this slightly plainer version...

The photo was done using Hev's Pollocks Toy Theatre, the figures of Lulu and El Nino which come from Heather's exhibition earlier this year, with our heads photoshopped in by me, then the whole thing stereoscopically photographed in Hev's pop-up photo booth and assembled by me. A team effort and no mistake.

Merry Christmas everyone.

See also this year's Kev F & Socks card

2017 - Kev F comic card, the Socks' card

2016 - Kev F comic card, the Socks' Shakespeare card

2015 - Kev F comic card, the Socks' Minging Detectives card

2014 - teasers for mine & the Socks' cards, I failed to put the finished things online!

2013 - Kev F schools card, the Socks don't seem to have had one

2012 - Hev & Kev's fairytale card (a classic, above), Kev F schools card,

2011 - Hev & Kev's and the Socks cards

2010 - Hev & Kev's card (below), and Kev F comic card

YOU ARE CORDIALLY INVITED TO

HEV AND KEY'S

*Being an early **evening**
of **pleasantries** for
one and **all**!
Bring **tipple** of choice
and **yourselves**.
Comestibles provided*

*Flat 2, 7 Leagrove Road
Clevedon BS21 7QR
RSVP to heathertweed@me.com
07931 810858*

**A SPLENDID TIME IS
GUARANTEED FOR ALL!**

**GENERAL
CONVIVIALITIES**

**GAMES
ENTERTAINMENTS**

SOIREE

SAT DEC 29

STARTS 4.30PM, ARRIVE BY 5.00 - CARRIAGES AT 10.30PM

Sunday, 30 December 2018
Death At The Circus - Murder
Mystery Party

Hev and I just threw our first
Murder Mystery Party for years,
and it was the biggest one ever.
Way back in the 90s we did quite a
few of these, writing parts for up to
8 guests, often getting them
dressed up. This time we just
extended a party invite to a larger
number of people (expecting a few
to cry off and have other
commitments at this busy time) and
wrote the parts accordingly,
handing them out to them when
they arrived. Most didn't know there
was a Murder Mystery element to
the party. Thing is, we'd anticipated
a few people not being able to
make it, and everybody could. So it
was that Hev and I wrote parts for
18 characters in our Circus based

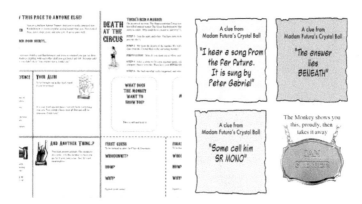

game - Death At The Circus. (Apologies to our friends who weren't invited, we really were trying to limit numbers, that was all). Here's the rather mammoth page they had to chew through over first drinks. -->

DEATH AT THE CIRCUS – Murder Mystery Dec 2018.

There has been a fire at The Hippocambrian Circus. It started in the animal cages and threatened all the animals. All have been saved except for the Animal Trainer THE GREAT BARTHOLOMEW and almost all of his Famous Performing Monkeys (one has survived). Bartholomew has been burnt to death, destroying any other clues on his person.

Once the fire has been put out we see that hidden beneath the monkey cages was the circus's safe, the location of which was a secret to most of the performers, as was the identity of the keyholder (while the boss was away). Because of the heat of the fire, the safe was too hot to touch or open.

An insurance policy has shown up, insuring the lives of the Performing Monkeys. The name on the policy has been burnt off.

There are no footprints leading up to the monkeys cage, despite it being muddy all around.

You all have individual notes with the secrets you know, suspect, or are hiding. Here are the facts we all know.

Then each person got their personal sheet to read, with secrets they knew, and their suspicions, like so...

In addition to these notes they got extra clues - a message from Madame Futura's Crystal Ball and a look at something the surviving monkey wanted to show them. These looked like this...

So, have you solved the crime yet? Don't worry, neither did anyone else at this stage. Each person got to ask one question, all of us gathered together in a group, then they wrote down and handed in their guesses. Nobody had the correct answer. Then we relaxed and partied for a bit, which is when the party started to sound like our usual entertaining event (Hev & I were worried that, rather than being an ice breaker, the Murder Mystery had led to a first half hour of everyone sat round silently). The party looked a bit like this (but really, you had to be there)...

Then after the food had come out we had the final round up. People got to compare clues with each other, then made their final guesses as to whodunnit, how and why. And this time, though 14 people got it wrong, two people (Chris and James) guessed the culprits, for widely varying and incorrect reasons. Here is the full selection of Crystal Ball clues, do they point to a killer yet?

I'd love to show you all the individual players' sheets, with all the different clues they had, but life's too short and I can't imagine anyone would ever read them all. So stop reading now if you don't want spoilers. Here is the explanation of the crime, as read

out by the surviving monkey (played on the night by me).

FINAL EXPLANATION

Hi, I'm a Performing Monkey. My name's Uncle Tom Cobley.

You know my fellow Performing Monkeys - Bill Brewer, Jan Stewer, Peter Gurney, Peter Davy, Dan'l Whiddon and Harry Hawke. We were called that after Widdecombe Fair. Cos our boss, The Great Bartholemew, came from Widdecombe.

And his brother, Stanley, named himself after the town. He called himself Widdecombe The Clown. Widdecombe the Clown is Stan Bartholemew, the Great Bartholemew's brother. That is, Jack Bartholemew's brother.

So on the night we were doing what we always do, nicking stuff off each other. The stuff we nick from the punters usually. And watching you lot, having your rows, and combing your horses and whatever. And playing with

fire. You all do that. The fire bloke taught you, and he even taught us. Dunno why, we couldn't see the point.

Fire bloke taught Bartholemew - he's the monkey who can't speak proper monkey - how to make fire come out of his trousers. Brilliant, we pissed ourselves every time. And he taught us some fire tricks, and we could never work out why. Breathe fire, throw fire, set fire, that sort of thing.

So we Monkeys nick stuff off each other, and there's nothing more valuable to us than these tags. They're called name tags. They're our treasure. Cos, well, they seem to mean a lot to everyone. I mean you lot. You do the ah-thing when you see the tags. "Aah". Don't know what the rest of what you say means, but it begins aah. We like aah.

So we were nicking tags. And, cut a long story short, I won. I got everyone's tags. And they're like, we want them back. And I'm like,

seriously, this has taken me all night. Then I remembered the fire tricks. So I torched them.

So I get to keep the tags. Look. I've got everyone's tags.

What's your problem? Let me explain, I torched everyone, so I win tags. That's A Good Thing. Cos I have All The Tags.

What bit of winning don't you understand? I've just beaten Bill Brewer, Jan Stewer, Peter Gurney, Peter Davy, Dan'l Whiddon, Harry Hawke - and Bartholemew The monkey who didn't speak proper monkey, and all -

(Sung) and Bartholemew The monkey who didn't speak proper monkey, and all.

-->
THE END

Sunday, 30 December 2018
Mum, 1936 - 2018
Sadly, but as you were no doubt expecting, Mum, Corral, finally gave up the ghost at around midday today, December 30th.

With her usual immaculate timing, and consideration for everyone else, she was able to see her Birthday on December 20th and Christmas Day, and leaves us when we (Jude and Kev) are around to sort things out for her.

Thankyou to everyone who's visited, sent the hundreds of cards and the thousands of kind words over the past few months while she's been here in the care home in Kibworth. Hers has been a rapid decline since she had to move out of the family home in August, with her still able to draw and finish her Christmas card in October before she really started to fade.

Though she's never been a fan of cliches, I think she'll allow us to say she passed away quietly in her sleep and was feeling no pain.

News of funeral arrangements will come soon, when we know more. Corral wouldn't want you to be sad or maudlin and we think she'd rather you raised a glass to her at Hogmanay, share fond memories of her, and have a Happy New Year when it comes.

Love from Jude and Kev

Monday, 31 December 2018
My Comic Strip Review Of 2018

In the nick of time, here it is. My annual comic strip review of the year. Hope it doesn't look too maudlin in black and white. To be honest, I didn't have time to finish it in full colour so I opted for monochrome. As you can probably see, the image in the bottom right hand corner had to be changed from a picture of The Knoll, described as Mum's new home, to a picture of Mum herself, who timed it nicely and squeezes in as the final and biggest news of the year.

The last few months saw me moving out of my office of 16 years and working from home, with mountains of stuff currently in storage, at the same time as Mum was moving out of Windmill Gardens, her home for 50 years (we moved in in 1968, how perfect and anniversorial was that?), and into the Knoll care home for, it turned out, a little over four months.

The Socks had a good year, with Superheroes being another hit show at Edinburgh, followed by an interesting nine day run in Denmark doing a mixture of Superheroes and special Brexit shows. And I had another bumper year of comic art, drawing The Story of Joseph

	2018	'17	'16	'15	'14	'13	'12	'11	'10
School days	103	96	92	117	120	97	82	124	109
Flights (return)	15	21	14	7	14	18	12	23	?
Socks shows	54	36	65	55	71	76	110	64	?
Caricature gigs	0	3	6	7	8	20	8	13	?
Nights away	tbc	66	90	90	79	74	123	?	?
Socks videos	50	25	56	41	37	55	81	36	79

and, with Book Of Ruth and Jael Wife Of Heber, completed my Women Of The Bible book, which we should see in the new year. And, yes, I know I've said that before. Some publishers move in mysterious ways.

103 of my days were occupied delivering Comic Art Masterclasses and similar things at schools, libraries, art centres, festivals and the like all over the world. From Switzerland to the Isle Of Wight, Hannover to Dublin, and all points in between (inc all countries of the British Isles, as per, from Falkirk to Felixstowe and Enniskillen to Neath).

I can't begin to imagine how many miles I drove and flew this year, but I can only apologise to the environment. Here's the table of the big stats of the year.

As for the year to come, all we know is it begins with a funeral on January 9th, after which surprises galore await I'm sure.

Happy New Year when it comes!

Kev F Dec 31st 2018

CPSIA information can be obtained
at www.ICGtesting.com
Printed in the USA
BVHW020401080519
547592BV00026BA/1328/P

9 780368 671524